*Say **YES** to a more Liberal Approach to Fiscal
Conservative Governance*

SMALLER
GOVERNMENT,
BIGGER PEOPLE,
STRONGER
SOCIETY

*Say **NO** to Profligate Unionised Socialist
Labour Class Warfare*

Anthony Weston Brewster

ISBN-13: 978-1508419877
ISBN-10: 1508419876

This book is dedicated to our children and young people whose behavior must be influenced by inspirational community leaders in this world of mixed messages. In Africa, the saying goes, it takes a whole village to raise a child and it should be no different here.

CONTENTS

Introduction

We suffered thirteen years of profligate unionised socialist New Labour governance, which spent too much of our national wealth and borrowed money on government bureaucracy, essential public services and dubious foreign wars and created a national debt mountain for their successors. During an extended period of economic growth, they should have built up financial reserves and 'fixed the roof when the sun was shining' ready for rainy days ahead. However, having spent so much of our national wealth and 'other people's money', they were unprepared for the banking crash (2008) and the global recession (2008-12). Having wrecked our economy and having been voted out of office (2010) they then had the arrogance to leave a note for their successors apologising for running out of money!

If we are to create a better society for our children and grandchildren, we must say **NO** to economically inept unionised socialism, which inevitably wrecks our enterprise economy. On the other hand, we must say **YES** to a more liberal approach to fiscal conservatism, which supports a free market enterprise economy, limited government, balanced budgets and the need to 'live within our means'. We must, therefore, create smaller European and national governments and devolve more power to regional and local governments and much more power to the people they serve.

Having suffered remote European and national governments and having created more accountable regional governments and assemblies, there is now a need for the devolution of greater powers to regional and local governments, as local democracy has the power to unleash human potential that is not possible in any other way. When we have achieved the devolution of economic and taxation powers to more independent and accountable and transparent regional and local government, we can then turn our attention to a protracted process of education for responsible citizenship, more contemporary community policing and inspirational community leadership, which are the foundation stones for the ultimate goal of social improvement, community renewal and real social justice.

So far as education for citizenship is concerned, our community schools, which should produce fine young citizens ready for the world of work, concentrate too much on the national curriculum and too little on moral education, character training, socialisation training, vocational training and sporting excellence. Furthermore, government ministers spend too much time criticising the performance of some schools, which are often in the most challenging areas, which are doing their best to guide our young people through the world of education. It's difficult enough for teachers to maintain calm and disciplined classrooms, which are conducive with effective teaching and learning, without ministerial criticism, which can only be justified when those who criticise are above reproach themselves.

It is, therefore, essential that our elected representatives carry out their public duties with honesty, integrity, accountability and transparency, in the public interest. However, recent evidence suggests that many elected representatives, who were quick to criticise others, had themselves fallen below acceptable standards of probity and rectitude in carrying out their public duties, particularly relating to their expenses claims. Our elected politicians must restrain their personal greed and ensure that they lead their constituents by the 'power of example' not the 'example of greed'.

We must develop a contemporary approach to community policing, with more community constables, concerned with the prevention of criminal and antisocial behaviour, before it gets out of control and moves from the streets to the courts and the prisons, which are the 'universities of crime'.

A more contemporary approach to community policing would ensure that community constables are released from the bureaucracy of the criminal justice system and given the freedom to work as community activists and community organisers in the interests of crime prevention and reduction. They would work with natural community leaders to identify those young people who are on the low road to the courts and prisons and attempt to divert them to the high road of enterprise, opportunity and employment.

Furthermore, those executives who are responsible for the production and transmission of television programmes and films and videos and internet communications, appear to have no regard for moral and social standards. They accept no responsibility for the social damage caused by the casual use of crude, obscene and degrading language and gratuitous violence and aggression and the adverse effect it has upon our vulnerable young children and impressionable teenagers, who should be exposed to inspirational and motivational community leadership from their elders.

What sort of example are these people giving to our children and young people, with a constant diatribe of obscene and degrading language, disturbing aggression and violence, which is meant to reflect domestic reality? Do they really think that we all live our lives in a perpetual state of bad-tempered, foul-mouthed aggression and domestic violence?

The time has now come for the older people in our communities to stand up and be counted and provide inspirational community leadership to our vulnerable children and impressionable teenagers who are searching for inspirational leadership in a world of mixed messages. There is often an absence of inspirational community leadership from the older generation in many of our troubled communities, the very places which need mutual respect between the older and younger generations. However, when there is a vacuum of community leadership, the authorities must locate natural community leaders, from within the community, and provide them with the necessary support to raise the aspirations of the local people.

There also appears to be a lack of civic pride and community spirit and a decline in civilised behaviour in many of our communities, particularly in those areas which suffer the damaging effects of criminal and antisocial behaviour and the illegal and dangerous drugs epidemic. More than ever before, we must develop a social culture of moral education, responsible citizenship and community leadership. We need to encourage a renewed sense of community spirit and civic pride and we must show outrage at the violent street gang culture, the senseless binge drinking culture, the illegal drugs epidemic and the casual use of obscene and degrading language, if we are to reverse the decline in civilised behaviour.

Social duties are exercised best in local communities where it is easier for local people to make the transition from private interests to public duties. However, the draconian control of public finances by ministers gives them a degree of control over local councils which emasculated local democracy and creates a climate of apathy and indifference to the political process. A more liberal conservative approach to governance, should believe in the devolution of more power to regional and local government and local councillors on the basis of subsidiarity, which is the devolution of economic power to the lowest practical level.

The over-centralisation of economic and taxation power is a socialist practice which is a threat to our liberal democracy. The only way that real democracy can be achieved, is when the voters reject economically inept unionised socialism, which believes in state control, and accepts a more liberal approach to fiscal conservatism, which believes in limited government. This approach demands the devolution of more powers to regional and local government and town and community or parish councils and the need to get remote big government off the backs of local people.

A more liberal approach to fiscal conservatism believes in smaller and more efficient European and national governments and independent, transparent and accountable regional and local government. It also believes in a free market enterprise economy and fiscal discipline and balanced budgets and 'living within our means'. However, whilst the liberal tradition demands equality, liberty and social justice, under the Chancellor and Prime Minister, W E Gladstone (1809-98), in the late 19th century, they developed a public policy with low public expenditure, low taxation and free trade, which is similar to the conservative tradition. Furthermore, classical liberalism supports limited government and some contemporary liberals prefer a minimal welfare state, with a safety-net for the poor, provided by local government. It is thought that liberal and conservative values have much in common but that they both have little in common with divisive unionised socialist Labour 'class warfare' and the negative 'politics of envy', which should have no place in British politics.

We need a more permanent alliance of conservative minded Liberals and more liberal minded Conservatives, who oppose bureaucratic socialism, imposed by those who supported communism when younger. Incidentally, the Conservative and Liberal Coalition Government (2010) was not the first time the two parties had formed an electoral alliance. In 1886 ninety three (93) Liberal Members of Parliament forged an electoral pact with the Conservatives to win the 1887 General Election, which lasted twenty six years, when they merged to form the Conservative and Unionist Party.

The reality is that we are all socialist-minded, in so far as we seek to transcend class distinction, we are all liberal minded, in so far as we stand for freedom of the individual, and we are all conservative minded in so far as we distrust political ideology and wasteful bureaucracy and have a deep feeling for custom and tradition. Consequently, the Labour Party should have no monopoly over socialism and should not be seen as the sole representative of the working class, as many of their leaders are very comfortable with the trappings of the aristocratic House of Lords.

Former New Labour ministers, such as the Deputy Prime Minister, John Prescott, a champion of 'class warfare' rhetoric, missed the opportunity to remove all the hereditary peers, who are the pinnacle of aristocratic class distinction. What they achieved in their thirteen years in office was to remove some hereditary peers and replace them with themselves and their socialist supporters, who had the breath-taking hypocrisy to accept a life-peerage from the conservative establishment they had for so long schemed to destroy. What our egalitarian instincts demand is a 'no-class' meritocracy, not a 'political class' aristocracy, particularly one which consists of socialist 'class warriors' who practice the 'politics of envy' and hate upper-class privilege, unless they are the beneficiaries.

It is, of course, very convenient and dignified and lucrative for senior politicians to be elevated to the upper chamber when their main political careers are coming to an end. However, what we need is a smaller and mainly elected second chamber, which is accountable to the electorate and attracts distinguished business, professional and political leaders, who are qualified to amend primary legislation. A mainly elected second chamber would be much more acceptable to the public than the arbitrary elevation, to an exclusive aristocratic gentleman's and ladies club, of old socialist 'class warriors', who had spent a lifetime plotting the demise of the upper chamber and the 'privileged' hereditary peers, which can only be described as self-serving hypocrisy on a grand scale. Furthermore, the recent 'cash for honours' and 'cash for legislative amendments' scandals have done nothing for the reputation of the Right Honourable Lordships, which suggests that the second chamber is in urgent need of reform.

To make matters worse we have also been exposed to the parliamentary expenses scandal, with ministers and members, with their snouts in the expenses trough as they travelled first class on the Westminster gravy-train, followed by their Lordships in business class as one would expect. However, the ultimate expenses bonanza, yet to be revealed, is enjoyed by members of the profligate European Union (EU), as they travel 'club class' on the lucrative Brussels to Strasbourg Express.

However, the old and New Labour converts to political elitism, in their aristocratic Westminster bubble, are unlikely to vote to dismantle their lucrative 'retirement home' in the upper chamber, which is the ultimate symbol of class distinction, as 'turkeys don't often vote for Christmas'.

We must now move away from the unionised socialist Labour approach of over-centralisation, over-regulation, over-taxation, over-spending and debt creation, which always ends in tears. We must move towards a more liberal fiscal conservative approach to governance, which supports an enterprise economy and the principle that you've got to 'earn it before you spend it'. However, fiscal conservative governments always have to adopt a more authoritarian approach, to sort out the economic mess left by unionised Labour, such as the embarrassing 'Winter of Discontent'.

Just imagine a more liberal fiscal conservative government without the suffocating burden of deficit and debt reduction, which they inevitably inherit from big-spending Labour. Just imagine, if they could inherit a balanced budget, how they would energise our enterprise economy and stimulate employment and build more efficient and effective government services and welfare support, a safety net for those in genuine need. The fiscal Conservatives would always 'fix the roof when the sun was shining' and would always build up financial reserves for the 'rainy days' ahead.

However, we have now reached the end of the weary road to the socialist 'dream factory' and we are again enduring a period of economic turmoil, in response to quite severe austerity measures, imposed by a liberal fiscal conservative coalition government, in response to a miserable economic performance by a profligate unionised socialist New Labour government.

They cannot, of course, expect any support from the Labour opposition, who are in denial about their contribution to our dire economic straits. This includes former New Labour ministers, who had actually worked in the Treasury, such as the leader of the Labour Party, Ed Miliband, and his Shadow Chancellor, Ed Balls, who were both economic advisors to the Treasury and Chancellor of the Exchequer, Gordon Brown. Whilst they were both very significant players in the decisions which led to our economic decline, such as our unsustainable debt and our unaffordable welfare and our uncontrolled immigration, they disingenuously criticise the coalition partners, as they attempt to get these things under control.

Many voters may now feel more at ease with a more liberal approach to fiscal conservatism, through a coalition government, despite public sector budget cuts, now that the economy is improving and there are more private sector jobs and we are reducing annual budget deficits as a precursor to reducing the national debt and 'living within our means'.

However, it will take many years of prudent fiscal conservatism to get our country back on its feet, before we get another profligate socialist Labour government, which will be in denial about the damage they always do to our country. The weary electorate should now realise, after decades of inept unionised socialist Labour economic mismanagement, that it is the economic discipline of prudent fiscal conservatism which will stimulate commercial enterprise and generate wealth to finance the public sector.

We need smaller and more efficient, European and national and regional governments, which do 'fewer things better' as 'governments should only do for the people what they can't do for themselves'. We need politicians and bureaucrats to delegate their work on the basis of subsidiarity, which is devolving power to the lowest practical level and closer to the people.

However, smaller more efficient government and essential public services will not happen under big-spending socialist Labour, it can only happen under a more prudent fiscal conservative approach to governance, which instinctively believes in fiscal discipline and balanced budgets. However, we can't have a 'one party state' regardless of their political persuasion.

It is, therefore, essential that socialist old or New Labour becomes less reliant on their socialist trade union leader paymasters and emerges as an independent social democratic party, which believes in a free market enterprise economy and resists the persistent habit of spending more than we earn as a nation, to finance their grateful 'client state' beneficiaries.

However, an independent social democratic party is unlikely to happen, as the Unite Union leader, Red Len McCluskey, has promised to fund the Labour Party in the general election campaign, which will further bind them to their trade union leader comrades and paymasters. He has also threatened to disaffiliate his union from the Labour Party and launch a 'Socialist Workers Party' if they fail to win the 2015 General Election.

We must, therefore, support a more liberal fiscal conservative approach to governance, which believes in fiscal discipline, balanced budgets, efficient public services, affordable welfare and 'living within our means' and not expanding essential public services with 'other people's money'.

We can then devolve more economic and taxation powers to regional and local government and then turn our attention to education for responsible citizenship, more contemporary community policing and inspirational community leadership and the ultimate objective of social improvement, community renewal, real social justice and more power to the people.

CHAPTER 1:

We Need Fiscal Conservatism NOT Profligate Socialism

Don't give the keys to the people who crashed the car

This book was written when New Labour was creating a national debt mountain legacy and updated when the more prudent Conservative and Liberal Coalition was reducing public sector spending and stimulating private sector growth. The author was always concerned about the dire economic record of unionised Labour and always favoured a more liberal approach to fiscal conservatism and a free market enterprise economy.

It was always intended to illuminate the road to social improvement, community renewal and social justice through education for citizenship, more contemporary community policing and inspirational community leadership. However, we must first deal with the national debt mountain, created by the excessive spending and borrowing of unionised Labour administrations, which always leave our country in dire financial straits.

This book was not intended to be a political tome beyond the need to dismantle the socialist big-state and devolve political and economic power to more accountable and transparent local government and town and community or parish councils. However, the reality is that the last New Labour government was obsessed with centrally imposed league tables and arbitrary targets and maintained a 'Stalinist' control over compliant local government, destroying any hope of local democracy.

Thirteen years of New Labour unionised socialism demonstrated that big-spending socialists have an adverse effect upon their own egalitarian ambitions for social improvement, community renewal and social justice. They expanded government bureaucracy, public services and welfare dependency and engaged in dubious foreign wars, well beyond our ability to finance them from national income. They created unsustainable annual budget deficits and overall national debt, keeping nothing for a rainy day, and were not prepared for the 2008 banking crash and global recession.

Whilst we were enjoying an unprecedented period of economic success, profligate New Labour embarked on a reckless tax, borrow, spend and waste binge. Rather than investing taxation revenues into more efficient government and more effective public services and more affordable welfare they expanded government bureaucracy, public services and welfare, creating their very own client state with other people's money.

As we watch the coalition partners struggle to reduce public sector spending and stimulate private sector growth and withdraw from very expensive wars and reduce the national debt burden, who will challenge the myth that it was all the fault of the 'greedy bankers' and reveal that it had much to do with the inordinate growth in socialist Labour spending?

There is, of course, a dramatic difference between profligate socialism and fiscal conservatism, which is highlighted by the dire state of public finances when old Labour left office in 1979 and when New Labour left office in 2010, as opposed to a balanced budget when the more prudent Conservatives left office in 1997, which emphasises the consequences of profligate socialist largesse as opposed to prudent fiscal conservatism.

The consequences of profligate socialist largesse and growing national debt, under New Labour, was that the new coalition government had to rebalance a weak economy and suffer the obstruction of the opposition and their militant trade union leader comrades. The only way to achieve enduring social justice is to build an enterprise economy that can provide economic opportunity and only the private sector can make that happen.

However, it is obvious that no new government can get such excessive borrowing, spending, waste and debt under control in one term of office. Excessive public spending on government institutions, public services, welfare entitlements and expensive foreign wars, produces recurring annual budget deficits, which are added to the overall national debt. These debts require servicing long after those responsible have left office and perversely creates an opportunity for those responsible for the debt to disingenuously blame consequent austerity cuts on their successors.

Many will remember the embarrassing 1970s when socialist old Labour were under the influence of their militant trade union leader paymasters and we suffered the dreaded 'Winter of Discontent' and were seen as the 'Poor Man of Europe'. They will remember that rubbish bins were not being emptied and dead bodies were not being buried, which resulted in a landslide victory for the Conservatives, which had a public mandate to reform the loss-making nationalised industries, such as steel, coal, rail, cars and ships, which were wholly dependent on government subsidies.

In 1976 the Labour Government under Prime Minister James Callaghan faced a sterling crisis, during which the value of the pound tumbled and the government found it difficult to raise sufficient funds to maintain its socialist spending commitments. The Labour Chancellor Dennis Healey was forced to apply to the International Monetary Fund (IMF) for a £2.3 billion rescue package which was the largest ever call on IMF resources at that time. In November 1976 the IMF announced its conditions for a loan, which included deep cuts in public expenditure, effectively taking control of our domestic policy, which was seen as a national humiliation.

When the Conservatives won the 1979 General Election, with their leader Margaret Thatcher, they inherited from incompetent unionised socialist old Labour, a 'poisoned chalice' of unreformed loss-making nationalised industries and widespread industrial strife, agitated by extremely militant socialist trade union leader barons. We were in serious financial and commercial difficulties and we were seen as a 'basket case' economy.

The Conservative Government inherited an annual budget deficit of £9.4 billion in 1979, which they turned into an annual budget surplus of £3.9 billion in 1988 and then £4.2 billion in 1989 before the Exchange Rate Mechanism (ERM) debacle of 1992 (our failed attempt to join the Euro) and a period of recession, when the annual budget deficit exploded to £50 billion in 1993. The Conservatives then worked to reduce the annual budget deficit to £15.6 billion in 1997, when they lost the general election and New Labour stormed into power and Prime Minister Blair told the nation that a 'new dawn had arrived' and 'things could only get better'.

New Labour promised, in their general election manifesto, to stick with the Conservative spending plans should they win the election. Having won the general election and having stuck to their promise, they turned the annual budget deficits into an annual budget surplus of £0.7 billion in 1998, £12.6 billion in 1999, £16.7 billion in 2000 and £8.4 billion in 2001. However, the big-spending socialists then increased the annual budget deficit to £69 billion by 2008 and a massive £156 billion by 2009, after the 2008 banking crash and the start of a serious global recession.

According to the Institute of Fiscal Studies, New Labour inherited public finances which were improving due to substantial tax increases and cuts in public spending which were implemented by the prudent Conservatives since 1993 and whilst New Labour stuck to the Conservative spending plans between 1997 and 2001 by the eve of the financial crisis in 2008 we had one of the largest structural budget deficits in the developed world.

The Conservative and Liberal Coalition Government took office in 2010 and were faced with a tide of recurring annual budget deficits of £148.6 billion in 2010, £120.6 billion in 2011 and a growing national debt and introduced 'severe' cuts to public sector budgets, which were normally opposed by Labour who were in denial about their fiscal incompetence.

Despite the Labour opposition to budget cuts, imposed by the coalition partners, the Chancellor announced in his 'Autumn Budget Statement' on 5 December 2013 that the budget deficits were expected to reduce to £111 billion in 2013/14; £96 billion in 2014/15; £79 billion in 2015/16; £51 billion in 2016/17; £23 billion in 2017/18 and a small surplus in 2018/19. Furthermore, on 14 March 2014 the independent Office of Budget Responsibility (OBR) published the public sector net borrowing figures (annual budget deficits) for the period 2010/11 to 2014/15 as follows; 2010/11 £134 billion; 2011/12 £112 billion;

2012/13 £110 billion; 2013/14 £98 billion and 2014/15 £87 billion. According to EU limits, public sector net borrowing (annual budget deficits) should not normally exceed 3% of our Gross Domestic Product (GDP) per annum.

The independent 'Office of Budget Responsibility' (OBR) published the UK net borrowing figures, as a percentage of GDP in September 2014, which started shortly after New Labour took office in 1997 as follows:

In 2000/01 there was an annual budget surplus of 3.9% of GDP, moving to a 0.2% deficit in 2001/02, then to 2.5%; then to 3.0%; then to 3.5%; then to 3.6%; then to 2.5%; then to 2.6% and to 6.9% by 2008/09.Whilst the subsequent figures were affected by the banking crisis (2008) and the global recession (2008-2012) the annual budget deficit grew to a peak of 11% in 2009/10; then 9.3% in 2010/11; 7.6% in 2011/12; 7.4% in 2012/13; 6.5% in 2013/14 and a forecast of 5.5% in 2014/15; 4.2% in 2015/16; 2.4% in 2016/17; 0.8% in 2017/18, then into budget surplus.

The following are the public sector net borrowings from the Chancellor's Autumn Statement of 3 December 2014. The public sector net borrowing or annual budget deficit was expected to be £97.5 billion or 5.6% of GDP in 2013/14; then £91.3 billion or 5.0% of GDP in 2014/15; then £75.9 billion or 4.0% of GDP in 2015/16; then £40.9 billion or 2.1% of GDP in 2016/17; then £14.5 billion or 0.7% of GDP in 2017/18; then an annual budget surplus of £4 billion in 2018/19 and £23.1 billion in 2019/20.

Whatever anyone says about the Conservatives in government, they are consistent in their attempts to reduce recurring annual budget deficits (spending more than we earn as a nation) to achieve an annual budget surplus (spending less than we earn as a nation) and then make a start to reduce the national debt mountain and start to 'live within our means'.

After a long period of financial restraint by the Conservatives, who were attempting to reduce the national debt accumulated by old Labour, and a short period of financial restraint by New Labour, which had promised to conform to the Conservative spending plans, prior to the 1997 General Election, the national debt reduced to 29% of Gross Domestic Product (GDP) by 2002. However, under profligate New Labour, despite a period of economic growth, the national debt increased to 36.4% of GDP by 2007/8 and to 56.8% of GDP by July 2009, mainly due to increased spending on health (NHS), education and social security.

The website 'Economics Help' had this to say about the New Labour years in power:

"Given the period of strong economic growth, it is not surprising that Labour wished to increase spending on health care and education… a critic would point out that… running budget deficits during an unsustainable economic boom was irresponsible. In retrospect Labour would have been better reducing the public sector (net) debt further. This would have given the government more room for manoeuvre during the crisis of 2008 -12. Also with growth strong, this was the best time to reduce the budget deficit (and) given the high growth in the 2000s it would have been better to be stricter with public spending."

New Labour should have been more responsible and should have 'fixed the roof when the sun was shining' to be ready for the inevitable 'rainy days ahead'.

However, despite the election of a new government (2010), subsequent to the banking crash and start of the global recession, and the introduction of 'severe' cuts to public sector budgets, the national debt continued to rise to 68% of GDP by July 2011 and to 86.8% by the first quarter of 2012 and was forecast to rise to 95.6% by 2013 and 98.7% by 2014.

So far as the national debt is concerned, the following are the public sector net debt forecasts, as a percentage of our Gross Domestic Product (GDP) from the Chancellor's Autumn Statement of 3 December 2014; 78.8% of GDP in 2013/14; and forecast to be 80.4% in 2014/15; 81.1% in 2015/16; 80.7% in 2016/17; 78.8% in 2017/18; 76.2% in 2018/19 and 72.8% in 2019/20. According to EU limits, public sector net debt should not normally exceed 60% of a country's Gross Domestic Product (GDP).

When New Labour came to power in1997 the national debt was £352 billion, which reduced to £337 billion (2000) and then increased to £527 billion (2007/08) and £902 billion (2010/11) before the new Conservative and Liberal Coalition Government could start to reduce public spending.

In May 2010, when the coalition partners came into power, the national debt was £890 billion, which according to New Labour would continue to rise to £1,400 billion by 2014/15 (includes an estimate for the potential impact of bailing out the banking sector). In July 2011 the national debt was £940 billion or 68% of GDP, which rose to £1,278 billion or 86.8% by the first quarter of 2012 and forecast to rise to 95.6% in 2013 and 98.7% in 2014. However, by the end of 2013, under the coalition cuts to public service budgets, the national debt was £1,254.3 billion or 75.7% of GDP and by the end of June 2014 it was £1,304 billion or 77.3% of GDP and expected to peak at 79.9% in 2015/16. Furthermore, according to the National Debt Clock (www.nationaldebtclock.co.uk) on 31 December 2014 at about 10.50 a.m. the national debt was £1,471,574,000,000 and growing at a rate of £5,170 per second. This enormous national debt amounted to £23,635 debt per citizen and £46,653 debt per taxpayer.

This rising tide of national debt was created by the

inordinate spending on the public sector by New Labour and made considerably worse by the banking crisis (2008) and the subsequent global recession (2008-2012). It was certainly not created by the coalition partners who were not in power when the crisis started. Whilst the coalition partners attempted to reduce the annual budget deficits, through public sector budget cuts, the task is made more difficult due to the recurring nature of spending commitments, started before they came into office. It is also made more difficult by the attitude of the militant trade union leaders, who instinctively oppose any reduction in public sector budgets. The irony of this situation is that those who increased spending on the public sector and created the recurring annual budget deficits and growing national debt are then in denial about their contribution to the deficits and debt and generally vote against any measures by their successors in government to reduce public spending.

So on what do we spend our money and how difficult will it be to turn the tide? In 2009-10 we spent £195.5 billion on welfare, rising to £202.6 billion in 2010-11. Public finances are dominated by welfare, which includes pensions, tax credits, unemployment, sickness, housing, council tax, child support and other benefits. In 2009-10 we spent £99.9 billion on the National Health Service (NHS), rising to £104 billion in 2010-11. We spent £66.4 billion on Education in 2009-10, rising to £69.2 billion in 2010-11.We also spent £42.9 billion on debt interest payments in 2010-11 which are forecast to rise to a significant £71.3 billion by 2017/18.

These figures were updated in the Chancellor's Autumn Statement on 3 December2014 and shown as the balance sheet; **Money In:** £27 billion in council tax; £27 billion in business rates; £41 billion in corporation tax; £47 billion in excise duties; £110 billion in national insurance; £111 billion in VAT; £118 billion other; £167 billion income tax, which is a total income of £648 billion. **Money Out:** £222 billion on welfare; £53 billion on debt interest payments; £53 billion other; £32 billion on public order and safety; £31 billion on personal social services; £25 billion on housing and environment; £23 billion on transport; £17 billion on industry, agriculture and employment; £98 billion on education; £38 billion on defence and £149 billion on health, which is a total spend of £732 billion. That's £648 billion income and £732 billion spending!

The above balance sheet, after almost five years of public sector budget cuts, shows the difficulty of any deficit and debt reduction strategy. The prudent Conservative approach is to reduce public sector spending and get into annual budget surplus and reduce the overall national debt and start to 'live within our means'. After almost five years in government and despite severe austerity cuts to public sector budgets we still have £648 billion income and £732 billion spending and a deficit of £84 billion and a growing national debt. Any government strategy to reduce public sector spending must include reducing the fraud and waste in the welfare budget of £222 billion. However, any attempt to reduce the enormous cost of welfare brings out 'bleeding heart' liberals and 'cradle to grave' socialists, who let their 'hearts rule their heads' and oppose any cuts. The principal message of recent years is that those who vote Labour are more than happy to 'live beyond our means' and create national debt and those who vote Conservative see the need to reduce the cost of the public sector and reduce the national debt and start to 'live within our means'.

The enormous cost of welfare, health and education raises the question of the viability of the 'free movement of people' principle within EU member states. When they expand into countries with weak economies, the burden falls on those EU countries with strong economies. Whilst it is important to support the weak economies and help them towards economic growth, they must demand that the people remain in their home country for an extended period, to actively support a regeneration programme.

However, those people who do move to another EU country must be able to support themselves and their families through productive employment or return to their country of origin. We also have people moving from the poorer countries to the richer countries and find there is no work and become homeless and they must be returned to their home country where they will be more secure, closer to their families and friends.

We also have a problem of active foreign criminals taking advantage of the free movement of people across member states to the detriment of the receiving country. The EU must see the necessity to return these active foreign criminals to their country of origin, where they are known to the authorities, rather than moving the crime burden to the receiving country.

Whilst we appear to be a rich country and are expected to be able to deal with any influx of immigrants and asylum seekers, we are not as rich as it seems. We are told that the state accounts for about 61% of the economy in Scotland, 73% in the North East of England, 77% in Wales and 81% in Northern Ireland. Furthermore, the cost of running the public sector has increased dramatically over the years. In 1930 the public sector was 28% of the economy and the private sector 72%. In 1960 the public sector was 36% and the private sector 64%. By 2012 the public sector had expanded to 52% of the economy and the private sector contracted to 48%, which can only be reversed by serious reductions in public sector expenditure.

The New Labour Chancellor squandered our national wealth and abused the nation's credit card on increases in public service jobs and pensions, and welfare dependency.

He also built new hospitals, schools and roads, using the very expensive 'off balance sheet' Private Finance Initiative (PFI) scheme. He was creating national debt well beyond our ability to service the debt from what we earned as a nation. He also sold off our gold reserves between 1999 and 2002 at the bottom of the market and lost about £13 billion at August 2011 prices, leaving little in reserve. He also raided the private pension schemes and destroyed one of the best private pension schemes in the world and damaged the pension expectations of thousands of responsible people who were saving for their retirement.

Does anyone really know the cost of our wars in Afghanistan and Iraq, besides the tragic deaths and serious injuries to thousands of soldiers and civilians and the displacement of refugees? Whilst smooth talking Prime Minister Blair was always able to justify his disastrous decision to take us to war against Saddam Hussein, on the grounds of national security, despite there being no weapons of mass destruction, he had no idea of the likely financial and human cost to our country. Furthermore, did Prime Minister Blair and his cabinet ministers have any idea how long the wars would last and how many casualties were likely to happen and how much the wars would cost the nation, including the medical costs of supporting wounded soldiers, and whether we could actually afford their decision?

According to Whitehall (June 2010) the cost of the Iraq war was £9.24 billion and the cost of the Afghan war was revealed by the Commons Library at £17.3 billion to the end of March 2012, on top of regular defence spending since 2001 and was expected to reach £20 billion by they handed over combat operations but what was the real cost of these wars, taking account of the future medical costs of wounded veterans?

Whilst the financial cost of the foreign wars is important, it pales into insignificance when compared with the tragic deaths and serious injuries suffered by so many soldiers and civilians. According to the Iraq Body Count, there were 4,587 civilians killed in Iraq in 2012 after the US troop withdrawal in 2011. There were also 9,571 civilians killed in 2013. On 12 November 2014 there was between 132,290 and 148,877 civilian deaths recorded in the Iraq conflict and 202,000 including combatants.

Despite the massive death toll, to release Iraq from a brutal dictator, the country is now being overrun by the barbaric jihadist Al-Qaeda affiliate known as the Islamic State (IS), which is brutally imposing an Islamic Caliphate in Iraq. Caliph is the name assumed by the successors of the prophet Mohammed and a Caliphate is the government of a Caliph.

Furthermore, the British military costs are minimal when compared with the USA. The 'National Priorities Project' Northampton MA, estimated that the cost of the two wars (1 May 2013) at $1,435,947,000,000, with Iraq costing $810,444,000,000 and Afghanistan $625,503,000,000 and growing rapidly. Even worse than the financial cost, on 26 February 2013 the Pentagon said that 6,596 USA troops had been killed in both wars and 49,746 seriously injured but no mention of civilian casualties!

Those who took us to war in Iraq, particularly Prime Minister Blair and Chancellor Brown and their compliant cabinet colleagues, should have a very heavy heart and the legality of their decision under international law should come under increasing scrutiny in the years ahead. Incidentally, Sir Ken MacDonald (now Lord MacDonald) a former Director of Public Prosecutions, told the Iraq War Inquiry: *"It is now very difficult to avoid the conclusion that Blair had engaged in an alarming subterfuge with his partner Bush and went on to mislead and cajole the British people into a deadly war they had made perfectly clear they did not want."*

Wouldn't it be refreshing if the Labour Party had the humility to admit that their leaders had misled the country over the reasons for going to war in Iraq and that the war had radicalised a generation of young British Muslims, which was the opinion of the former head of MI5?

We also need to ask ourselves why so many young British born Muslims have joined the barbaric jihadist Islamic State (IS) terrorist group in both Syria and Iraq, which commits so many vicious atrocities and brutally beheads infidels or non-believers in the name of Islam or Allah!

The controversial war against Saddam Hussain, which was opposed by millions of people, resulted in the resignations of two senior government ministers, who criticised their own government in their publications, *The Point of Departure* by Robin Cook (2004), 'The most damning account of Britain's decision to attack Iraq' and *An Honourable Deception* by Clare Short (2005), about 'New Labour, Iraq and the Misuse of Power'. Robin Cook wrote:

"I left because I could not support a war based on a false prospectus and waged without any international authority."

Clare Short wrote:

"I am afraid that I still find it impossible to brush aside what has happened. I believe the deceit profoundly dishonours Tony Blair and makes him unfit to hold the office of Prime Minister. The failure of the Labour Party to hold him to account... dishonours the party and especially the Parliamentary Labour Party..."

Despite this critical assessment of the dubious political

leadership of Prime Minister Blair, he was later inexplicably appointed the Middle East Peace Envoy by the UN, the EU, the USA and Russia (June 2007) prior to a period of increasing turmoil in the Middle East. How could the United Nations approve the appointment of one of the principal architects of the controversial Iraq war, which killed and seriously injured so many innocent civilians, including women and children, creating an army of displaced people, searching for sanctuary throughout the world?

It's so easy to start expensive foreign wars but it's so difficult to keep spiralling military costs under control. It's so easy to sell off our gold reserves at rock-bottom prices but it's so difficult to build them up again, as the value of gold increases. It's so easy to create public sector jobs and pensions but it's so difficult to rebalance a debt-ridden economy from public sector wealth consumption to private sector wealth creation.

The reality is that unionised socialist Labour always increases public sector jobs and wages and pensions and expands welfare dependency, creating their very own client state, financed through private sector wealth creation and borrowing. Socialist Labour governments always ignore the consequences of their insatiable appetite for spending on the public sector which is a wealth consumer and their grudging support for private sector enterprise which is a wealth producer and debt reducer.

Incidentally, this was not the first time that Labour had wrecked our enterprise economy and was kicked out of office for a lengthy period and the Conservatives had to bring government spending under control. They were kept out of office for fourteen years after 1931, thirteen years after 1951 and eighteen years after1979. Having again wrecked our economy (1997-2010) and been rejected by the electorate, their partisan approach to opposition suggests that they are in denial about their contribution to our debt-ridden society and choose to blame it on the 'greedy bankers' and a global recession, rather than their profligate economic ineptitude.

Having lost the 2010 General Election, the contestants for the Labour leadership showed no remorse for the economic mess left by the New Labour project and under pressure from Labour activists and militant trade union leaders, declared their support for socialism. This included the Miliband brothers, who were brought up in a Marxist household, with their father Ralph Miliband, a Marxist theorist, who was born in Brussels in 1924 (the eldest child of Polish and Jewish immigrants, who had left Warsaw after the First World War) and their Polish born mother, Marion Kozak, a well-known figure on the left of the socialist Labour Party.

In 1972, after many years as a Senior Lecturer in Political Science at the London School of Economics, Ralph Miliband moved to Leeds University where he was Professor of Politics. He was described by the Observer as a 'leading intellectual of the new left and an influential figure in shaping students and other attitudes' and was the author of many books including *Parliamentary Socialism* and *The State in Capitalist Society* and co-editor of the *Socialist Register*. This raises the question, to what extent did their parents socialist views shape the political opinions of their two sons, who were both ministers in the New Labour moderate pretence?

The surprising winner of the Labour Party Leadership contest was the younger brother Ed Miliband, whose limited work experience included a brief period as a television journalist, then a political speech writer and researcher and then an economics advisor to Chancellor Brown. He was later elected as MP for Doncaster North in South Yorkshire in 2005, then appointed Climate Change and Energy Secretary of State and later won the Labour Party leadership contest, due to the support of the trade union leaders. However, the majority of MPs and Labour Party members voted for his older and more experienced brother David. It would be better if our once proud country was led by politicians, with a long track-record of inspirational leadership, in a professional or commercial environment, rather than inexperienced academics, who've never had a proper job, outside the narrow confines of partisan politics but can talk for England.

The new leader of the Labour Party, who was named 'Red Ed' by the media, declared an end to the New Labour project and the start of a 'new generation' and claimed that he was not under the influence of their trade union leader paymasters and that there would be no lurch to the left. He had, however, achieved the leadership of the party, having promised the trade union paymasters that he was very much a socialist. However, the constitution of the new shadow cabinet suggested that the new generation description was misleading, as they were very much part of New Labour, such as Harriet Harman, Yvette Cooper, Ed Balls, Hilary Benn, Peter Hain, Douglas Alexander, Tessa Jowell, Andy Burnham, John Denham and Liam Byrne. Whilst some of them had been principal architects of the New Labour economic mismanagement, they would now have to package their economic approach to accord with the 'new generation' description, such as being converts to reduced public spending and balanced budgets.

At the same time as we witnessed the election of the 'new generation' of Labour Shadow Ministers, we were exposed to the nauseating spectacle of the former Prime Minister, Tony Blair, launching his memoirs entitled *The Journey*, having been preceded by his former spin-doctor Alastair Campbell with his many extracts from his diaries, starting with *The Blair Years*; then his former confidant, Peter (now Lord) Mandelson, with *The Third Man*; then the last New Labour Chancellor, Alistair Darling, with *Back from the Brink*; then the former Home Secretary, Foreign

Secretary and Justice Secretary, Jack Straw, with *Last Man Standing*; then former Chancellor and Prime Minister, Gordon Brown, with *Beyond the Crash*; then his minder Adrian McBride with *Power Trip: A decade of policy, plots and spin*. These publications revealed the deep divisions within the New Labour project, which was consumed with internal conflict, particularly the immature, festering relationship between Prime Minister Blair and Chancellor Brown, resulting in the resignation of the Prime Minister and the elevation of the Chancellor.

It would appear that the champagne socialist Prime Minister Blair, now a seriously wealthy, property owning multi-millionaire, who was the acceptable face of the New Labour project, operated as the front man for the former Neo-Marxist Chancellor Brown, who squandered the wealth of our nation from the treasury bunker, as we plunged ever deeper into an economic black hole of unacceptable and unsustainable national debt.

During an extended period of economic and commercial success, a more responsible Chancellor would have reduced our habitual reliance upon 'other people's money' and start to 'live within our means' and generate financial reserves in anticipation of an inevitable economic downturn, not create the ludicrous impression that he had done away with boom and bust and then be confronted with a financial crisis and global recession.

However, the main concern for the future is that four of the principal architects of the failed economic policies of New Labour are the Leader of the Labour Party Ed Miliband and his Shadow Chancellor Ed Balls (who were both economic advisors to the Treasury and the Chancellor) and the Shadow Home Secretary Yvette Cooper, a former Chief Secretary to the Treasury, and the hapless Liam Byrne, who left a pathetic note for his coalition partner successors, apologising for running out of money!

It is, therefore, very interesting to note the promises of senior Labour politicians, when they are seeking re-election, as opposed to their actions when in government. The Shadow Chancellor Ed Balls, a recent convert to balanced budgets, pledged that they would achieve a current budget surplus by the end of the next parliament should they be returned to power. Furthermore, the Shadow Chief Secretary to the Treasury Chris Leslie said that they must embrace the goal of balancing the books, as the foundation of successful public service provision is the sound stewardship of public finances. It's just the usual empty rhetoric to mislead the public.

So we are now expected to believe that those committed socialists, who could be in charge of the public finances, in a future Labour government, will be converts to the concept of balanced budgets and budget surpluses, when their depressing track record in government suggests the opposite.

Incidentally, whilst Labour shadow ministers are now self-styled converts to balanced budgets, they have not lost their appetite to increase the size of the public sector, which must be paid for from private sources. They have promised to raise £2 billion a year from a 'Mansion Tax' on the rich, which they will spend on more NHS nurses and doctors, which will increase the cost of the health service and the public sector pensions.

Furthermore, as we approach the 2015 General Election, there is now a rush by the Labour leadership to introduce new policies to reassure those with short memories that Labour can be trusted with the economy. Their leader, Ed Miliband, has promised to cut the budgets of most Whitehall departments every year until the nation's books are balanced and has promised a 'tough but balanced' approach to clear the deficits by the end of the next parliament. Only the National Health Service and Overseas Aid will escape the cuts. He proposes to cut the annual budget deficits by 'sensible spending cuts', not 'slash and burn', without putting key public services at risk. As usual, he ventured into 'class warfare' rhetoric, when he suggested that the Conservatives will look after the wealthiest people and everyone else will be on their own and public services will not be there when you need them. He said that the contrast between them and the Conservatives is that they won't take risks with our public finances or public services. Naturally, their long track-record suggests the opposite.

To illustrate the importance of prudent fiscal conservatism, as opposed to profligate unionised socialism, when it comes to balancing the nation's books, we should consider the experience of a liberal or socialist minded Democratic President (USA) who came into power in 2008 and turned a federal debt of about \$9 trillion into a debt of about \$18 trillion by 2014, which is spiralling out of control. However, a number of conservative Republican State Governors, who inherited large annual budget deficits, turned them into annual budget surpluses and simultaneously reduced the unemployment rates, according to the USA, Bureau of Labour Statistics.

For instance, the Republican Governor of Florida turned a \$3.6 billion budget deficit into a \$1.3 billion surplus and reduced the unemployment rate from 10.9% to 6.2%. The Republican Governor of Wisconsin turned a \$3.6 billion budget deficit into a \$1.6 billion surplus and reduced the unemployment rate from 7.7% to 6.1%. The Republican Governor of Ohio turned an \$8 billion deficit into a \$1.5 billion surplus and reduced the unemployment rate from 9.1% to 6.5%. The Republican Governor of Texas turned a \$5 billion deficit into a \$2.6 billion surplus and reduced the unemployment rate from 6.00% to 5.7%. Finally, the Republican Governor of South Carolina turned a \$700 million deficit into a \$160 million surplus and reduced the unemployment rate from 10.5% to 5.7%.

The above is a massive endorsement for fiscal conservative governance and a massive rejection of 'big spending' liberal-minded Democrats who let their 'hearts rule their heads' and create unsustainable national debt.

Incidentally, whilst the New Labour, Chancellor, Alistair Darling, had planned to implement austerity cuts to the public services and increase Value Added Tax, had they won the 2010 General Election, having failed to do so they claimed that the coalition austerity cuts were cutting 'too deep' and 'too fast'. They also called for an increase in public borrowing for investment, which would further increase annual budget deficits, national debt and debt interest payments. However, when the 'too deep' and 'too fast' mantra lost its electoral appeal, they changed to a 'cost of living' crisis, when much of the cost of living increases related to energy and food prices, which are normally outside of government control.

This disingenuous partisan criticism by the socialist Labour opposition merely encourages their public sector union leader comrades to take industrial action against the coalition government, which damages the recovery. Should the militant public sector union leaders continue to take strike action, in response to the coalition government's public sector budget cuts and pension reform, they will create a hostile climate, which is not conducive with investment, growth and private sector jobs, repeating the mistakes of the past, such as the 1984/85 miners' strike.

The militant socialist leaders of the National Union of Mineworkers (NUM) tried to bring down an elected Conservative Government in the 1984/85 miners' strike and terminally damaged the mining industry, rather than achieving a slower pit closure programme with civilised non-partisan negotiations. Whilst the socialist miners' union leaders were trying to protect their members' jobs, they chose to ignore the geological and economic arguments in favour of pit closures which were inevitable.

Furthermore, whilst they were again trying to bring down a Conservative Government, they ignored the fact that the pit closure programme was produced by the management of the National Coal Board (NCB) and was part of a long-term pit closure programme, which had seen many more uneconomic pits closed under Labour than under the Conservatives.

To put things into perspective, in early 1984, the Conservatives and the NCB announced plans to close a further 20 uneconomic pits (NB: The disclosure of government papers under the 30 year rule reveals that the NCB favoured the closure of 75 uneconomic pits) which led to the year-long miners' strike, which ended with the miners defeated. History will record that the old Labour socialist Government of the 1960s closed pits at the rate of one per week. Between 1965 and 1970 they closed 223 pits and the Wilson/ Callaghan Labour Governments closed 32 pits between 1974 and 1979. When the NCB announced plans to close a further 20 pits in the early 1980s it was the continuation of an historical trend, not a malicious and vindictive Conservative attack on hard working miners.

Why would any government throw thousands of hard working miners onto the unemployment register and have to pay out unemployment benefits, if it was not absolutely necessary? It just doesn't make sense.

It also needs to be said that Prime Minister Thatcher inherited a coal industry in 1979 that was in decline. In 1947 there were 750,000 miners working in over 800 pits but by 1983 there were just 240,000 miners working in about 190 pits and contrary to common belief the Conservative Government did attempt a rescue mission. In 1981 they provided a £50 million subsidy to British industries prepared to switch from cheap oil to expensive British coal. They then injected a further £200 million into the declining coal industry. Furthermore, companies which had gone abroad for coal, such as the Central Electricity Generating Board (CEGB), were banned from bringing coal into the country and 3 million tonnes piled up at Rotterdam at a cost of £30 million per year to the tax payer. By then the coal industry was losing £1.2 million per day. Interest payments amounted to £467 million for the year and the NCB needed a government grant of £875 million. By 1984 it cost £44 to mine a metric ton of British coal, whilst America, Australia and South Africa were selling it on the world markets for £32 per metric ton. British tax payers were subsidising the mining industry at a cost of £1.3 billion per year and that does not include the cost to taxpayer funded industries, such as steel and electricity, which were forced to buy British coal. Falling production, employment and sales and increasing subsidy was the reality of the coal industry inherited by Margaret Thatcher.

Sadly, the bitter miners' strike created a massive political and social divide, which culminated in many former mining communities actually celebrating the death of the former Prime Minister, Margaret Thatcher, whom many thought had saved our country from militant socialist trade union power. However, many others believe that she was responsible for the destruction of the mining industry and proud mining communities.

Whilst the Conservatives stayed in power until 1997 and managed to turn the ailing economy around and left the New Labour government with a balanced budget, the next thirteen years of profligate New Labour saw the creation of a public debt mountain and an imbalanced economy in the form of a burgeoning public sector and a contracting private sector.

The best way to stimulate economic growth and create private sector jobs is for governments to create an economic environment in which business owners have the confidence to expand their businesses with the support of the banks. It is enterprising business people who create business growth, private sector jobs and taxation revenues, which are used to finance government institutions, essential public services and welfare support, not government ministers, who often have meetings about meetings.

Whilst the coalition Chancellor said that he had no option but to introduce austerity cuts in response to the parlous state of the public finances left by New Labour he said that the majority of the cuts would fall on those with the broadest shoulders. He also said that he would reduce the burden on those at the bottom of the income ladder, which he did by raising the tax threshold, but that he must deal with the inherent abuse and fraud of the welfare system. However, any attempt to deal with welfare abuse and fraud, will be seen as an attack on the poor and will bring out 'bleeding heart' liberals and 'cradle to grave' socialists, who have no concern with the cost of welfare and the growing national debt.

Whilst public sector strike action, against public sector austerity cuts, will reduce investor confidence, business growth, wealth creation and tax revenues and increase the growing national debt, the informed electorate should support reductions in public sector funding, which are designed to achieve a balanced budget and ensure that we pay our way in the world.

However, we are now exposed to the partisan behaviour of the Labour opposition, who oppose any reductions in public spending, as we search for the road to economic recovery. The public must decide whether they are acting in the national interest or in their own self-interest. It's easy for the opposition to criticise the rate and depth of the coalition austerity measures but they should accept that the coalition partners were not in power when the debts accrued and the economy declined. They should take a more mature non-partisan approach to the need for public sector and welfare budget cuts and public sector pension reform and a balanced budget or suffer the reaction of the more informed electorate when they present themselves at the next general election as a party of government.

All the public expected of the opposition was a degree of contrition for their excessive borrowing and spending and the maturity to work with the coalition partners to reduce public sector budgets and reform public sector pensions and reduce annual budget deficits, the national debt and debt interest payments, in the national interest. If they could have come to terms with their persistent economic incompetence and have worked with the coalition partners, in a spirit of compromise, in the national interest, they could have changed their reputation for economic incompetence and may have improved their electoral credibility, in the minds of the voters.

We have already seen the reaction of the partisan trade unions and their members when they marched the streets of London in opposition to the austerity measures and we saw the anti-capitalist faction break from the otherwise peaceful demonstrations and attack the police and the high street banks and prominent commercial premises. It would be interesting to know how many of the anti-capitalist vandals were in employment and how many were reliant on social security benefits and were effectively biting the benevolent hand that feeds them. Don't they realise that the high street banks are an essential part of our enterprise economy?

However, the public should now take a more balanced approach to the austerity cuts, having watched the many violent street protests and the soup kitchens in the Greek tragedy, played out on our television screens, where the people are in denial about their parlous economic state. They would, of course, be virtually bankrupt without the financial support of the European Central Bank (ECB), the International Monetary Fund (IMF) and their European

Union (EU) partners, especially the Germans. They were a very low tax economy and had been living well beyond their means since joining the EU, yet many of their citizens were not prepared to accept the austerity medicine, being dispensed by their EU partners.

Consequently, the Greek voters have elected a radical left-wing party, which has promised to end austerity and renegotiate the terms of their 240 billion Euro bailout package, with the EU and IMF, which they say is stifling recovery. However, this radical approach could lead to further economic uncertainty.

The British public must also accept that thirteen years of financial incompetence, under the pretence of the New Labour brand, means that we were also living well beyond our means. The public must accept that we had no choice but to rebalance our economy away from public sector wealth consumption to private sector wealth creation and to reform our public sector pensions and to reduce our recurring annual budget deficits and to accept that it cannot happen overnight. No new government can reverse such a debt-ridden economy in one term of office, because of the recurring nature of annual budget deficits, which are added to the debt.

We should not let Labour shadow ministers create the false impression that our economic crisis can be turned around in one term of office, when it is more than obvious it will take at least a generation, as it did when the last old Labour Government left office in 1979. When New Labour increased public spending, they used borrowed money, which increased annual budget deficits and national debt. Much of the increased public spending, which creates annual budget deficits, was recurring public expenditure, which is added to the growing national debt, as opposed to exceptional spending or discretionary spending, which is not repeated.

The coalition government, faced with recurring annual

budget deficits and growing national debt and debt interest payments, had no choice but to reduce public sector spending, to enable them to reduce annual budget deficits, before they can reasonably start to reduce the growing national debt and debt interest payments. However, the opposition disingenuously criticised the coalition government, because the national debt was still growing, when they knew that the coalition could not start to reduce the overall national debt until the recurring annual budget deficits were turned into surplus, which could only be achieved by reductions in public spending, which would seriously damage their re-election chances.

Furthermore, no new government can reduce recurring annual budget deficits by public sector austerity measures, when they are persistently obstructed by militant public sector trade union leaders, resisting any reductions in public sector budgets and any reductions in public sector jobs and any (long overdue) reform of public sector pensions, which are becoming increasingly unaffordable due to an increased life expectancy.

However, despite the obstructive approach of the opposition and their trade union leader paymasters to the coalition agenda, we were told by the Office for National Statistics (ONS) in June 2013 that there was 22.8 million private sector workers employed in June 2010, which rose to 24.1 million by June 2013, which was a record number of people employed in the private sector. During the same period the number of public sector jobs had dropped from 6.3 million to 5.7 million. The 3 December 2014 Autumn Statement from the Chancellor said that the UK had a record high in employment of 30.8 million, which was 1.7 million up since 2010. UK employment had increased faster than any other country in the G7 and the economy had grown by 3% in the third quarter of 2014.

We must reject big spending unionised Labour socialism, which believes in state control, as the rot always starts at the top. We must encourage voters to embrace a more liberal conservative approach to governance, based upon limited central and regional government and the devolvement of more powers to local government and local people on the basis that democracy always grows from the bottom-up and dies from the top-down.

Whilst liberalism and conservatism may have a different approach to politics, a more liberal fiscal conservative approach would ensure that we support an enterprise economy and use reasonable taxation revenues to provide more efficient public services and more affordable welfare, a safety net for those in need. However, a coalition between 'cradle to grave' socialists and 'bleeding heart' liberals would increase taxation revenues and depress commercial enterprise and redistribute too much of our national wealth to their 'client state' and 'dependency culture'.

It is essential that any responsible government demonstrates economic discipline and balanced budgets and sensible welfare provision on the basis that as a respected nation we must 'live within our means'.

If the electorate reject a more liberal approach to fiscal conservatism at the next general election (2015) and reinstate unionised socialism under Labour, the architects of our economic demise, our country is doomed to further economic turmoil. Ironically, after thirteen years of New Labour socialist largesse, which submerged us in humiliating debt, their 2012 Party Conference mission statement was about 'Rebuilding Britain', which smacks of hypocrisy. Furthermore, despite their divisive 'class warfare' rhetoric, their 2014 marketing headline was about 'One Nation Labour', which suggests that they want to bring the nation together.

If anyone has any doubt as to why we got into financial difficulties under New Labour, as we had done under old Labour, consider the views of the former, self-proclaimed 'prudent' Chancellor, Gordon Brown, in the introduction to his 'Red Paper on Scotland' published in 1975 as follows:

"The public control of industries essential to the provision of social needs and services – the priorities being building and construction, food and food processing, insurance and pensions; the industries essential to the planning of services vital to the economy – the priorities being energy as a whole, land, banking and foreign trade; industries whose monopolistic position threatens the ability of society to plan its own future – the priorities being the taking over of the assets of the major British and American multinationals and industries essential to regional development – shipbuilding and textiles being obvious."

Furthermore, according to Tom Bower in his book *Gordon Brown, Prime Minister* published by Harper Perennial in 2007, as a university student he advocated more nationalisation of industry, a planned economy and the destruction of the ruling classes and that capitalism had failed and the private ownership of industry was hindering the unfolding of the social forces of production. Bower suggested that Gordon Brown's cure was a form of neo-Marxism.

Whilst the Labour Party was formed by the trade unions (1906) to ensure parliamentary representation for the workers, we must not allow them to claim that they have a monopoly on socialism and sole representation of the working class. The political representatives of the working class in a liberal western democracy should be in favour of free market capitalism, an enterprise economy and entrepreneurial endeavour, which provides employment opportunities and generates wealth to finance government institutions, essential public services and social welfare support.

Regrettably, every time socialist Labour is voted into power, they spend too much of our national wealth and borrowed money on big-government and bloated public services and welfare entitlements and create a debt mountain for the next prudent Conservative Government to sort out.

Even under the pretence of New Labour, which emerged from the ashes of old Labour and their militant trade union comrades and the dreaded 'Winter of Discontent', when we were described as the 'Poor Man of Europe', they still managed to wreck our economy, despite the prudent Conservatives having almost turned the old Labour debt into a surplus.

However, the leader of the Labour Party promised a complete change of approach in his speech to the Confederation of British Industry (CBI) in November 2014. He said that the next (Labour) government will face a huge challenge in bringing down the deficit, balancing the books and reducing the debt and creating a budget surplus. He also said that there would be no money for the next Labour government to spend but made no apology for the last New Labour government, of which he was an integral part, which left our country in a financial mess. Finally, he said the next Labour government would be about 'big-reform' not 'big-spending'.

So as we approach the 2015 General Election, having previously rejected incompetent socialism, under New Labour, which left our once proud country in economic turmoil, we must now support a more liberal fiscal conservative approach to 'living within our means' and ignore the empty promises of socialist Labour, who are desperate to get back into power.

There is, however, one main obstacle to the return of a more liberal fiscal conservative government, which is the growing public concern over our membership of the European Union (EU) and the associated economic and welfare migration, which puts pressure on our public services. These genuine concerns have increased the popularity of the United Kingdom Independence Party (UKIP), which opposes our membership of the EU, which will take votes from the Conservatives, who want to reform the EU, and could return another pro-European socialist Labour Government.

The main question, therefore, is which of the two main political parties, which are likely to form a government, have the policies to deal with the growing public concern about uncontrolled immigration which is putting our public services under so much pressure. We must first separate the economic immigrants from the EU, who come to our country under the authority of the 'free movement of people' and those who come from elsewhere. We must also separate them from asylum seekers, from the many war-torn countries around the world and countries with deplorable human rights records, seeking refuge in our liberal western democracy. We must always remember that the way to judge a civilised society is the way they treat strangers or foreigners, particularly those seeking asylum.

The Prime Minister, David Cameron, has promised the British people that he will renegotiate our relationship with the European Union and offer an in-out referendum on our continued membership, should he win the next general election. He has avoided a challenge to the principle of the 'free movement of people' which would have been unlikely to succeed.

He has chosen to attempt to reduce the numbers of economic immigrants by making our generous benefits system less attractive to those who come from the poorer countries, with derisory benefits. However, he is fighting an uphill battle as the extent of the immigration problem suggests that may people will support UKIP which claims that the only answer to the immigration problem is for us to leave the EU as the 'free movement of people' principle is non-negotiable and that changing the benefits system will not be a sufficient deterrent to those immigrants seeking a better life.

To understand public concern about economic and welfare immigration from the EU and elsewhere, which includes asylum seekers or refugees, Lord Andrew Green of Migration Watch recently suggested that before the New Labour Government, net migration was 50,000 per year. During the New Labour administration (1997–2010) net immigration peaked at 320,000 per year and it's now an average of about 250,000 per year, which has put an enormous strain on our essential public services.

Lord Green said that we need temporary relief from the 'free movement of people', which is a basic principle of our membership of the EU. He also said that southern European youth unemployment is astronomical and that's why they come here for jobs. However, so far as Eastern Europe is concerned, particularly Romania and Bulgaria, he suggested that they come here because their standard of living is about a quarter of ours. When asked what would be an acceptable level of net immigration he suggested 70,000, which means we could receive 120,000 immigrants, on the basis that an average of 50,000 British citizens leave every year.

We were recently informed by Oxford University's respected Migration Observatory, based on an analysis of the official 'Labour Force Survey', that more than a quarter of a million Romanian and Bulgarian nationals now live in Britain, a figure that has risen by almost 50,000 in the past year. The numbers are equivalent to a town the size of Wolverhampton.

When we wonder why so many East Europeans come to our country often for low-paid work, the following wage comparisons from 'Open Europe' suggests the answer. A Polish low-paid worker with no children would get a minimum wage of £114 per week in Poland. In the UK the same worker would get £290 per week, consisting of the minimum wage and working tax credits. Even taking away the working tax credits he would get £197 per week. There is no wonder there are so many EU nationals registered for National Insurance numbers in the UK. The following are the numbers who registered for National Insurance numbers in the year to June 2014; Romanians 103,000 which is up 468% on the previous year; Bulgarians 31,000 up 205%; Polish 98,000 down 7%; Spanish 46,000 down 9% and Italians 45,000 up 16%, which is a total of 323,000.

So far as employment is concerned the Office of National Statistics (ONS) reported that in the year to June 2014 there were 2.9 million non UK nationals employed, which is an increase of 9%. They also reported that 1.7 million EU nationals were employed, which is an increase of 16%.

However, to keep things in perspective, the Department of Work and Pensions (DWP) recently announced that 11.7% of those on jobseekers allowance and 5.8% of those who claim incapacity benefits are non UK nationals and of the 5.3 million who claim working age benefits 395,000 are non UK nationals. We have very little information about the numbers of immigrants who are in receipt of the myriad of other welfare benefits.

The EU bureaucrats should recognise these serious economic and social challenges and introduce conditions on the 'free movement of people', from the poorer to the richer countries, in accordance with their capacity to absorb them. This 'free movement of people' from the EU is in addition to asylum seekers from elsewhere, where there are so many internal wars and human rights abuses and vulnerable displaced people seeking refuge.

Opponents of the 'free movement of people' within the EU are often labelled as xenophobic, which means a fear or hatred of strangers or foreigners, which is disrespectful to those who consider it is important to effectively manage mass immigration and its huge social consequences.

Incidentally, the socialist New Labour Government (1997-2010) had the opportunity to restrict the influx of economic migrants from the expanded European Union in 2004 but chose to lift controls on Eastern European migrants, one of the very few countries in the European Union to do so.

They estimated or guessed that less than 13,000 migrants would come to the UK each year but the numbers were nearer 130,000 per year and that's a conservative estimate. The former New Labour, Cabinet Minister, Jack Straw, recently admitted that it was a 'spectacular mistake' for the New Labour Government to throw open its borders in this way, when most (sensible) EU countries retained controls for a further seven years.

Whilst managed immigration can produce significant economic benefits, uncontrolled immigration of those who often don't speak English and may not have the same cultural work ethic can put an intolerable strain onto essential public services and can lead to social unrest and feelings of xenophobia from the indigenous population. New Labour probably saw the East European economic migrants as a discreet form of social engineering, which would benefit their socialist cause, as they had grown up in a communist state and would be unfamiliar with conservatism or liberalism. Their decision to remove the restrictions on East European migrants was certainly not as innocent as a 'spectacular mistake'.

There is also some concern at the increasing cost of our membership of the European Union, which has almost doubled in the past five years. Our net contribution to the European Union project, which was born out of our entry into the European Economic Community (EEC) or

Common Market, was £4.6 billion in 2007; £3.3bn in 2008; £4.3bn in 2009; £7.4bn in 2010; £8.1bn in 2011; £8.5bn in 2012 and a massive £8.6bn in 2013.

This book is about creating smaller, more efficient government and bigger, more confident people, through a more liberal fiscal conservative approach to governance. However, this will not happen as long as we continue to elect profligate unionised socialist Labour governments, which always wreck our economy. Neither will it happen if the cost of our membership of the EU continues to increase and economic and welfare immigration continues unabated. Furthermore, whilst we might promote a more liberal or compassionate or social approach to fiscal conservative governance, which may appeal to a much wider electoral audience, most newly elected Conservative governments have no choice but to adopt a more authoritarian approach, to sort out an economic mess, caused by big spending unionised socialist old or New Labour governments.

A more liberal minded fiscal conservative approach to governance would demand smaller European and national and regional governments 'doing fewer things better' and 'living within their means' and independent, and transparent and accountable local government, working with the people.

The principal message to the UK electorate, therefore, is that we have suffered the politically adept and economically inept socialists, under the pretence of New Labour, and whilst the coalition government has had to re-establish fiscal discipline and dispense austerity medicine, we must not now open the flood gates for another big-spending Labour tsunami.

A similar message must go out to the USA electorate who voted for two terms of politically adept and economically inept democratic socialism, under President Obama, a former community organiser, the ultimate adversarial campaigner, with a socialist spending agenda, on the back of a slow economic recovery and a burgeoning national debt mountain.

By 2014, after six years of Obama style democratic socialism there were 15,000,000 more people on 'Food Stamp' entitlements, 5,000,000 more people on disability entitlement, 10,000,000 more people on free health care through Medicaid and 8,000,000 more people on unemployment insurance. Many Republicans believe that the Obama social democratic approach is to fashion a permanent democratic majority by making so many more people dependent on the government for their livelihood.

What we need in our free market enterprise economy and liberal western democracy is a more liberal fiscal conservative approach to governance, which, through the taxation system, stimulates enterprising entrepreneurs to generate business growth, private sector jobs and taxation revenues to fund more efficient government institutions and essential public services and welfare benefits, which are a safety-net for those in greatest need.

We also need to consider the words of John Mackay, the CEO of Whole Foods Supermarkets (USA), and Raj Sisodi, in *Conscious Capitalism*, published by Harvard Business School Publishing Corporation in 2014, who said:

"Every business has the potential for a higher purpose besides making money. Doctors have a higher purpose, they heal people, teachers educate people, architects design buildings and a business creates value for everyone with whom it trades; value for customers, employees, suppliers, investors and value for the larger community. Business people are truly the heroes, they are the value creators in the world (and) they lift humanity out of poverty and create prosperity."

We must respect our free market enterprise economy,

which creates employment opportunities and generates taxation revenues to finance government services and should be seen as altruistic capitalism and the basis for social improvement, community renewal and social justice.

The conservative ideology in democratic countries normally embraces the liberal principles of a free market economy, limited government and the rule of law. The political concept of liberal conservatism has come to be seen as just conservatism, prompting some conservatives who embrace stronger classical values, to call themselves Libertarians. However, in many countries, which have liberal conservative movements, the terms liberal and conservative are synonymous. Often this involves free market economics, a belief in individual responsibility, the defence of civil rights and the environment, support for a limited welfare state, lower taxation and minimal state intervention in the economy.

Whilst coalition governments are inevitable in the future, they are known to be indecisive. The Conservatives should, therefore, adopt a liberal fiscal conservative approach to governance and rebrand themselves as a Conservative Democratic Party (CDP), which would attract conservative minded Liberals, or form an alliance with the Liberal Democratic Party.

We also need unionised socialist Labour to put an end to their financial dependence on their militant trade union leader paymasters and become an independent Social Democratic Labour Party (SDLP), as he who pays the piper always plays the tune. The public must be governed by elected representatives, not by militant socialist trade union leader barons.

However, whether we have a liberal fiscal conservative approach to governance or a more independent approach to democratic socialism, we must reduce the suffocating power of the EU and UK governments and increase the power of regional and local governments and make them more independent, transparent and accountable to the people they serve.

The recent failed attempt by the Scottish Nationalists to break away from the United Kingdom resulted in a promise of the devolution of economic and taxation powers to the Scottish regional government. The referendum on Scottish independence was an expression of frustration by the Scottish Nationalists to remote governance from Westminster, particularly by the Conservatives, when the majority of Scottish voters, particularly in the industrial heartlands, support a more socialist approach to governance through the Scottish Labour Party or the Scottish Nationalist Party.

However, the promise of the devolution of more economic and taxation powers to Scotland has created a similar demand from the other regions, which cannot now be ignored. Whilst regional governance has brought politicians closer to the people they serve, we must now give more powers to much more independent, transparent and accountable local authorities and town and community or parish councils, as local democracy has the power to unleash human potential that is not possible in any other way.

A call must go out to the politicians to create smaller and more efficient European and national governments and bigger and more independent regional and local governments, which are accountable to the people.

CHAPTER 2:

We Need Smaller Government and Bigger People

Local democracy can unleash human potential which is not possible in any other way

When the New Labour government, which was dominated by Scottish cabinet ministers, devolved political and economic power to their Scottish homeland and to Wales and Northern Ireland, they added another layer of bureaucracy and further reduced the power of local government. The reality is that we need much smaller national and regional government 'talk-shops' and more independent, transparent and accountable local government and town and community or parish councils, to reduce public apathy towards remote government and unaccountable politicians.

So how can the fertile soil of local communities produce a rich harvest of local democracy, with community minded citizens involved in local government and town and community or parish council administration, when it needs cabinet ministers to release their political and economic stranglehold over local government? Such a change was always unlikely to happen under socialist Labour governments which practice 'top-down' economic micro-management of local government administration.

We must, therefore, increase the independence of local government and town and community or parish councils, giving them the power to make decisions without constant reference to regional or central government. The national and regional governments must legislate for local authority tax-raising powers to enable them to accept devolved responsibilities and become more independent and transparent and responsive to the people.

Amitai Etzioni, who wrote a book entitled *The Third Way to a Good Society*, said in *The Times* on 5 July 2000:

"The government does best when it allows communities that are intact, much more decision making freedom. Where communities have frayed, the government can help reactivate them by training local leaders and ensuring safe public places. Communities do not happen in private homes and cars but in spaces people share. The third way must pay more attention to society and the institutions that make people better members of society."

The following extract from *The National Wealth* by Dominic Hobson, published by Harper Collins in 1999, argues that the centralisation of power has had a damaging effect upon the process of local democracy:

"Central government supplies four in every five pounds spent by local government. This gives Westminster and Whitehall a degree of control over expenditure and activities of councils which emasculates local democracy. Local Government is no longer an expression of civic

pride or a laboratory of democracy. Indifference to local government means that three out of five voters do not turn out in council elections. In some inner-city wards less than one in ten people bother to vote."

Former socialist government ministers had very little understanding of the management principle, to delegate responsibility and authority with confidence to the lowest practical level. This gives local managers and supervisors the confidence to use their discretion and initiative to get things done, rather than spending too much time agonising over central and regional government imposed rules and regulations, bureaucratic red tape, arbitrary targets, performance measurements and league tables, which reduces their discretion, initiative and effectiveness.

Whilst New Labour ministers would cite the devolvement of power to regional government and assemblies as their contribution to reducing the power of central government, they merely created an additional layer of bureaucratic 'talk shops' between central and local government, rather than devolving real economic power direct to local government.

So far as England is concerned, a more liberal fiscal Conservative approach to governance should consider a more federal approach to local government, giving them the power to raise their own finances. The Chris Blackhurst interview with Sir Merrick Cockell, former chairman of the Local Government Association (LGA), which represents 373 councils in England and Wales, said in *The Independent* on 4 August 2014:

"As chairman of the LGA he oversaw the 'Rewiring Public Services' campaign. The idea was to rejuvenate local democracy, restore civic pride, improve public services and boost economic growth. It was founded on ten propositions including: giving people a meaningful say on local taxes and spending; the creation of an

'England Minister' to fight... for a greater slice of government funding; reducing ministers ability to intervene in local decisions and using municipal bonds to pay for investment in infrastructure... He's passionate about devolution for England... England needs a greater say in how public money is spent..."

There is no doubt that enduring social improvement, community renewal and social justice will only emerge from independent, transparent and accountable local government administrations, working with local communities and business and professional people, social entrepreneurs, philanthropists and natural community leaders and will not emerge from the dead hand of bureaucracy. For the benefit of ordinary people, government must be conducted in small communities, with no one person becoming too powerful or being seduced by their own power.

The importance of local community leadership, rather than central government bureaucracy, was emphasised by Alexander Garrett in an article entitled 'Dynamic Leaders with a Social Conscience' published in the magazine *Management Today* in 2000, which said:

"We say it is individuals who make things happen, not committees. If you look at the most successful (local) community projects they are run by people with leadership qualities, not by committees. Good leadership, in whichever sector, involves handing over power to the people."

The concept of self-reliant communities was discussed in *Going Local, Creating Self-Reliant Communities in a Global Age* by Michael H Shuman, published by The Free Press (USA) in 1998, which said:

"A United States with thousands of additional small communities, each financed with progressive taxes, each empowered to govern creatively, each with inhabitants who know their neighbours, would be a powerful incubator for community corporations. Smart national and state politicians should see this kind of devolution, not as threatening their power but as freeing their level of government from social, economic and political problems that must be solved primarily at local level."

The following extract from *The Common Sense of Community* written by Dick Atkinson and published by DEMOS, 1994, under the heading 'The urban village and the active citizen' had this to say about the importance of local democracy in the form of non-party political Parish Councils:

"The emergent self-governing urban village needs its own non-party political voice and a degree of control over its own affairs. Parish councils have a legal existence. Those rural villages which have retained these interesting forms of local democracy elect their own parish councillors to represent their own very local concerns. The Parish Council is able to levy a precept on the council tax which can give the parish councillors a useful income to spend as they and their constituents see fit."

The social cohesion of local communities would be improved if taxation revenues could be levied by local authorities and town and community or parish councils, as opposed to just central government.

The book *Decent and Indecent, our Personal and Political Behaviour* by Doctor Benjamin Spock and published by Penguin Books Limited, in 1972, under the heading 'To make the citizen more important again' had this to say on the spread of conurbations on democracy:

"A weakness in our democracy, as our cities continue to expand, is the sense of the citizen, that he is too small and powerless to count. It is high time that we were exploring ways to break up the cities into semi-autonomous neighbourhoods, in order to return to the citizen the sense not only that the community knows and cares about him but that he has an obligation to be co-operative with his neighbours and help guide the government. The neighbourhoods should be able to have at least partial control of schools, police and recreational facilities."

It would also be a good idea to delegate the responsibility for social security benefit payments to local authorities, which are closer to the local people and the economic, commercial and employment situation. They would be able to identify those citizens who need support and those who are 'playing the system' and have no intention of finding work and are more than happy to languish on benefits for the rest of their lives.

So far as the long-term unemployed are concerned, we must break their welfare entitlement mentality, even those who are virtually unemployable.

Local Authorities with the responsibilities of managing social security benefit payments would incentivise local businesses and public services and registered charities to employ long-term unemployed people in low-skilled manual or even administrative work. The Local Authorities would send all or part of the social security benefits to the new employer, who would pay the 'benefit worker' for full or part time work and the amount would be reduced for non-attendance, which is not supported by a sick note. The payments would probably have to be tax exempt. This method of benefit payment to the long-term unemployed would benefit the employer with an extra pair of hands at no extra cost and the 'benefit worker' with job training and work experience and renewed personal dignity.

The concept of 'benefit work' would be more difficult

to administer than a cheque in the post and leaving the recipient to go through the motions of job-seeking, including those who are virtually unemployable. However, it makes sense to get indolent people into the habit of working for a living, rather than relying on the taxpayer to fund their lifestyle. There would, however, be a cry of 'slave labour' from those who see benefits as an entitlement, even when the recipient has no motivation to work.

We must create more media interest in liberating localism, rather than their fixation on regional, national and international celebrity politics. We are consumed with their obsession with the European Parliament and Commission, the Westminster Parliament, the Scottish Parliament and the Northern Ireland and Welsh Assemblies, which are expensive political talk-shops, whilst they show little interest in local government matters.

It's difficult enough to communicate with our national and regional parliaments and assemblies, so what's the chance of transparency and accountability, should we become a federal state of an ever expanding European Union. Big is certainly not beautiful, it is remote, impersonal, obstinate, bureaucratic and unmanageable. So if we are concerned with the lack of transparency and accountability of our remote national and regional governments, we can no longer ignore the relentless 'glacial' movement of the European Union towards a more federal 'Super State'.

We must, therefore, demand that the politicians produce a European Union of independent nation states, with the devolvement of political and economic power to national and regional and local governments, on the basis of subsidiarity, which is making political decisions at the lowest practical level. New Labour ministers should have concentrated on the devolution of political and economic independence to existing local government, as opposed to the creation of a further layer of regional government. However, as we continue to watch the relentless expansion of the European Union 'Super State', we ignore the recent demise of the Union of Soviet Socialist Republics (USSR) and its command economy and dependent satellite states and the fact that socialism does not work.

If we want to retain responsive national, regional and local government administrations, we must fight to retain our economic and monetary independence and our parliamentary democracy, within a European framework of economic and commercial co-operation, which was the perception of the electorate when we voted to join the Common Market.

We should, therefore, consider Article 2 of the Treaty of Rome, 1957, which established the European Economic Community (EEC) as follows:

"The Community shall have as its task, by establishing a Common Market and progressively approximating the economic policies of member states, to promote throughout the Community a harmonious development of economic activities, a continuous and balanced expansion, an increase in stability and accelerated raising of standards of living and closer relations between the states belonging to it."

The British Prime Minister, John Major, signed the EU Maastricht Treaty in February 1992 and asserted that it involved relatively minor changes. However, the then EU Commission President, Jacques Delors, insisted that it was a major step towards a federal Europe. Whilst Britain was successful in removing references to the federal goal and including the importance of respecting the principle of subsidiarity the Treaty included a number of steps towards supranational integration such as the establishment of a new European Union citizenship. However, what they conveniently did not broadcast was that under the Treaty all citizens of the EU member states had the right to come and live in the UK (or any other member state) and enjoy all the rights and freedoms of the country.

The subsequent controversial Lisbon Treaty, which was ratified by the heads of state of the member countries and not, with a few exceptions, exposed to the electorate of those countries, authorised the election of a European Union President by the heads of states and not the electorate of those countries, which is not particularly democratic but is cost effective when compared with the USA Presidential Election campaigns. However, when one considers the very large number of member countries and their different languages, an electoral campaign would be extremely difficult, with a number of Presidential candidates and no common language. The Lisbon Treaty became law on 1 December 2009 eight years after the European leaders launched a process to make the EU 'more democratic, more transparent and more efficient'. However, opponents see the treaty as part of a federalist agenda which threatens national sovereignty.

However, the greatest assault on the democratic process was suffered by the electorate of the United Kingdom (UK), who were promised a referendum on the controversial Lisbon Treaty by the New Labour Government in their election manifesto, when they were seeking re-election, but having been re-elected, they reneged on their promise and ratified the treaty without reference to the disenfranchised electorate.

The biggest insult to the public was when Prime Minister Gordon Brown signed the Lisbon Treaty Ratification Document, after the official signing ceremony, despite widespread public disquiet, without having a public mandate as an elected Prime Minister, which is an unprecedented constitutional anomaly, which should probably have been revisited.

The EU Parliament and Commission should concentrate on global matters which affect all member states. They should concern themselves with the adverse effects of serious weather changes, resulting from global warming; about the recent damage to international banking and financial services and internet fraud; about the adverse effects of international criminal gangs and terrorism and about uncontrolled legal and illegal immigration on member states. They should continue to harmonise trading laws and conventions across the member states, which was the original intention of the European Economic Community (EEC) before it was reinvented and reconstructed by the political elite as the European Union (EU). In fact, it would be sensible to harmonise the language differences between the many member states in the European Parliament, which incurs massive expenditure on interpreters and makes it very difficult to conduct business. After more than fifty years they should now be able to talk to each other in one common language and that language should be English, which is the accepted business language of the world. The previous economic success of the USA must be down to the fact that they operate under one language, one currency and one fiscal policy. The recent financial crisis (2008) and global recession suggests that the EU can't continue with member states having their own fiscal policies. The pressure from the EU leaders is for member states to accept one fiscal policy and one central bank, which is the imposition of an EU 'Super State', a country called Europe, which will be difficult for the electorate of member states to swallow, assuming they are properly consulted.

For twelve years the European Union (EU) auditors have refused to endorse the spending on large parts of the EU budget. Whilst the auditors have found problems with the way the EU spends its money they have declared them to be 'reliable'. However, the European Court of Auditors

(ECA) said that the EU misspent about 7 billion euros (£5.5 billion) last year (2013) that's 4.7% of its annual budget. They also said the budget should be focused on achieving results, rather than on 'just getting funds spent'. The most error-prone spending areas in 2013 were regional policy, including energy and transport (6.9% error-rate) and rural development, including environment, fisheries and health (6.7% error-rate). They recently agreed an EU budget (2014-20) of 960 billion euros, which is the maximum that the EU can spend. The money allocated to the EU budget includes 325 billion euros to support those countries and regions that are economically lagging behind other member states and 278 billion euros to aid farmers and help maintain rural communities and a derisory 15.7 billion euros for the fight against international terrorism and dealing with asylum seekers and refugees, which seems inadequate.

So far as the United Kingdom (UK) is concerned, one of the first actions of the New Labour Government (1997), which was dominated by Scottish Cabinet Ministers, was to give Scotland a regional government, often run by the Scottish Nationalist Party (SNP), which is committed to Scottish independence; and to give Wales its own regional assembly, influenced by the Welsh nationalists (Plaid Cymru) who are committed to Welsh independence; and to give Northern Ireland its own regional assembly, influenced by Irish nationalists (Sinn Fein) and former leaders of the Irish Republican Army (IRA), who are dedicated to merge with the Irish Republic (Eire). This leaves the English the only net contributor to the UK finances with no regional parliament. If ever there was a recipe for the eventual break-up of the United Kingdom, it was the creation of devolved regional governments, which was the obsession of the former Chancellor and Prime Minister, Gordon Brown, when he was chairman of the Scottish Labour Party's Devolution Committee in 1978.

The domination of the United Kingdom Parliament by a divisive socialist New Labour Government, which was dominated by Scottish born cabinet ministers, served to make many English voters deeply resentful, not least because of their urgency to devolve power to their homeland of Scotland. This was the first nail in the coffin of the not so United Kingdom, which produced a Scottish Nationalist Party (SNP) Regional Government and their divisive demand for a Referendum on Scottish independence, which they achieved in September 2014. The result of the Scottish Referendum was that 45% of those who voted wanted independence and 55% voted to retain the Union, on an unprecedented electoral turnout of 84.6%.

The disproportionate political influence of Scottish born Prime Ministers and Chancellors of the Exchequer and Secretaries of State in the United Kingdom Government (1997-2010) should have been a matter of public concern. Their rush to introduce Scottish devolution, after their general election (1997) victory, was the catalyst for the leadership of the Scottish Nationalist Party (SNP) to demand a Scottish independence referendum. However, the vote was restricted to residents of Scotland, regardless of their nationality, which included thousands of foreign people living in Scotland, but did not allow the 750,000 Scottish born citizens, living in the rest of the United Kingdom, to vote on the future of their country.

Furthermore, when one considers what is known as the 'West Lothian Question', where Scottish constituency Members of Parliament (UK) are able to vote on legislation which affects only England, when English constituency Members of Parliament (UK) can't vote on legislation in the Scottish Parliament, which affects only Scotland, there appears to be a compelling case for an English Parliament, which would represent the vast majority of the population and electorate of the United Kingdom.

It was very convenient for Scottish Labour constituency members of the UK Parliament (MPs) to be appointed by the two Scottish born Prime Ministers, to become Secretaries of State and Ministers and Speaker of the Commons and chairmen of the most influential Parliamentary Select Committees, as they had little work to do in their Scottish constituencies, as the majority of the constituency work was done by Members of the Scottish Parliament (MSPs). In fact, the constituency workload of the Members of Parliament (UK) in the three regions must be so minimal, when compared with their English counterparts, due to the existence of the members of the three regional administrations, that their existence should be questioned on the basis of necessity and expense.

Furthermore, the English electorate are also faced with the spectacle of the 'Barnett Formula', which gives a higher financial settlement per capita to Scottish, Welsh and Ulster constituencies, than it does to English constituencies, which was produced many decades ago by the then Labour government minister, Joel Barnett, which was based upon varying perceived standards of poverty throughout the United Kingdom.

The English have quietly suffered consecutive New Labour Governments, which were dominated by Scottish Members of Parliament, occupying the principal offices of state. There were two Scottish Prime Ministers, two Scottish Chancellors of the Exchequer, two Scottish Lord Chancellors, a Scottish Speaker of the House of Commons, a Scottish Home Secretary, three Scottish Defence Secretaries and many more junior ministers. These appointments suggest that the Scottish socialist political elite are fiercely patriotic and favour their own countrymen in positions of political power.

This predominance of Scottish Ministers, running the affairs of the United Kingdom (UK) and in particular the affairs of England, is certainly not a recent phenomenon.

Between 1761 and 1767, twenty eight Scots achieved a high rank in the UK government under a Scottish born Prime Minister, John, Earl of Bute, who was seen as favouring his own kind. This was often the case in politics, the military and business throughout the British Empire. English political cartoonists of the time were savagely racist in tone, portraying Scottish born politicians as treacherous and greedy mendicants who were growing rich at the expense of the English.

The dominance of the Scots abroad was described in a book entitled *The Scottish Empire* by Michael Fry, published by Tuckwell Press (2001), which said:

"It tells of how the British Empire came to be dominated by the Scots and how it truly became the Scottish Empire."

Another book entitled *Scotland's Empire* 1600-1815 by T M Devine, published by Penguin Group (2003) said:

"The Scots had an enormous impact on the global development of the British Empire as emigrants, soldiers, merchants and colonial administrators."

The disproportionate influence of the immigrant Scots in Canada in the 19th Century was mentioned in the book *The Scottish 100: Portraits of History's Most Influential Scots* by Duncan A Bruce and published by Carrol and Graf Publishers (2000) which said:

"In 1700 the great fur-trading Hudson Bay Company had no Scots but by 1800 four out of five of employees were Scots and by 1900 the principal shareholders were Scots. Five of Canada's first six colleges were founded by Scots and two political groups were

controlled by Scots and dominated the politics... Though they formed one fifteenth of the population, they controlled the fur trade, the great banking and financial houses, the major educational institutions and to a considerable degree the government."

The irony is that the Scottish diaspora has often seen Scottish immigrants and their descendants achieve disproportionate political power abroad, yet the Scottish Nationalist Party (SNP) with their devolved parliament and government, demanded a referendum to break away from the United Kingdom (UK) Government, which had been dominated by Scottish politicians for most of the last two decades and we still have a Prime Minister, David Cameron, of Scottish descent! It should have been the English electorate who wanted to break away from the many Scottish Labour politicians who dominated the UK government, which includes England, the only part of the UK with no regional government.

Had the Scottish electorate voted for independence in the referendum (2014), it would have inflicted a terminal blow on the British Labour Party, which would have lost 41 Scottish Members of Parliament (UK) and would have struggled to get a majority in subsequent parliamentary elections (UK). It would, however, have had the opposite effect on the Conservative Party, as Scotland is effectively a Conservative free zone.

There are currently 41 Labour and 1 Conservative Members of the United Kingdom Parliament in Scotland and a vote for independence would have seen the Labour Party struggle to get a majority in what remained of the United Kingdom. The Labour Party 'Better Together' campaign was a desperate attempt to retain their UK Parliamentary dominance through their traditional network of Scottish constituencies.

Incidentally, a consequence of the Scottish

Independence Referendum, according to the polls, is that there is now more support for the Scottish Nationalists and less support for Scottish Labour, which has been in the process of changing its leader. Furthermore, an unintended consequence of the referendum campaign is that the Scottish Nationalists could now be much more influential in the next general election campaign and prevent the Labour Party winning enough seats in Scotland to achieve a majority in the UK Parliament. However, the Scottish Nationalists and the Labour Party could form a coalition or alliance to achieve a majority in the UK Parliament and produce another Scottish dominated UK Government, which would be similar to the New Labour Government (1997 – 2010).

On a similar basis, the nationalist fervour generated by the United Kingdom Independence Party (UKIP) could take electoral seats from the Conservatives and prevent them winning the 2015 General Election.

Furthermore, whilst UKIP may take seats from the Conservatives and make it difficult for them to win the General Election, they would have a problem forming a coalition or alliance with the Labour Party, which is pro-European Union and has not committed to an in-out referendum.

There is, however, no doubt that a resurgent Scottish Nationalist Party (SNP) may damage the Scottish Labour Party and increase SNP seats in the UK Parliament. This small country of about five million people will have a disproportionate influence in the affairs of the UK, with 63 million people, should they collude with the Labour Party. Consequently, they could fashion a permanent socialist coalition or alliance in the UK Parliament, within a socialist minded big-state European Union.

The solution to this anomaly, which is a consequence of the Scottish Independence Referendum, is for UKIP (which wants independence from the EU) to support the

Conservative Party (which wants fundamental EU reform and an in-out referendum) and form a coalition or alliance in the UK Parliament. The reality is that UKIP will not be in a position to form a government and provide a referendum in the foreseeable future. Their only hope is to form a coalition or alliance with the Conservatives, who want to negotiate reform within the EU or recommend withdrawal. The governance of the UK is, therefore, a battle between a Labour and SNP coalition, which would again ensure Scottish domination over the United Kingdom, including England, or a Conservative coalition with UKIP, which would seek to achieve EU reform or recommend withdrawal.

The ultimate prize for the governance of the UK is for the four regions to be virtually independent, with elected governments and parliaments and general elections. The four regions would then form a UK representative government, with an appointed prime minister, deputy prime minister and cabinet ministers, in direct proportion to the votes cast for each political party in the general elections of the four regional governments.

So far as England is concerned, the solution is for the English members of the UK Parliament, now known as MPs, to become English Members of Parliament (EMPs), who would work from the House of Commons chamber. So far as Scotland is concerned they could retain Members of the Scottish Parliament (MSPs) and dispense with Members of the UK Parliament (MPs) or vice versa. Similarly, Members of the Welsh and Northern Ireland Assemblies could be retained and dispense with Members of the UK Parliament (MPs) or vice versa. The political parties in the three regions, other than England, would have to decide which of the two members would represent the regional parliament and be a delegate to the UK Parliament, to avoid duplication and expense.

The House of Commons management would schedule

the work of the English Parliament and the UK Parliament in the commons chamber and the regions would send delegates to debate and vote on matters which affect the UK. This new arrangement would eliminate duplicity and cost in the Scottish, Welsh and Northern Ireland regions where they now have constituency members of the regional government/assemblies and UK Members of Parliament (MPs) who are covering the same ground.

The recent Scottish Referendum (2014) failed to achieve independence but got the promise of the devolution of economic and taxation powers to the Scottish Parliament and raised the question of more powers to the Welsh and Northern Ireland Assemblies and the demand for an English Parliament and devolution to English Regions or Local Authorities.

Whilst the coalition government has the responsibility to devolve more powers to the Scottish Government, they also need to do the same or something similar for the Welsh and Northern Irish Assemblies and consider creating an English Parliament and devolving more powers to an English Parliament and English Regions, through Local Authorities.

The first stage in this process would be to remove the duplicity of the UK Members of Parliament (MPs) in Scotland, Wales and Northern Ireland, who represent the same constituents as members of the three regional administrations. Each parliamentary constituency in the three regions should have the members of their regional parliament and no separate UK Members of Parliament (MPs). The members of the three regional administrations would sit in their regional parliaments and remove the name Assemblies, so far as Wales and Northern Ireland are concerned. The three regional parliaments would use their current voting system and the political parties with the most electoral votes would form the regional government with a First Minister, a Deputy First Minister and Ministers of State and there would be five year fixed term elections.

The second stage in the process would be to form an English Parliament and English Government in the House of Commons chamber and existing UK members of parliament (MPs) in England would become English members of parliament and be known as EMPs, to avoid confusion with members of the European parliament, who are known as MEPs.

The third stage in the process would be to form a new UK Parliament, operating from the Commons chamber, which would concern itself with matters affecting the United Kingdom (UK) and the European Union (EU) and other matters of an international or global significance and they must not interfere in the devolved responsibilities of the four regions.

This is an example of a government which should do fewer things better.

The current management of the House of Commons would have the responsibility to schedule the work of the new English Parliament and the new United Kingdom (UK) Parliament in the Commons chamber on the basis of say three (3) days per week on English Government matters and say two (2) days per week on United Kingdom Government matters.

To avoid duplicity of representation and unnecessary costs there would be no separate constituency members of the United Kingdom Parliament. The four regional governments would send their constituency member delegates to the United Kingdom Parliament to represent the views of the separate political parties represented in their regional parliaments. The management of the four regional parliaments would schedule the work of their own parliament and send their delegates to the UK Parliament.

The fourth stage in the process would be to form a representative United Kingdom government, as follows: The regional governments would have fixed term elections every five years. The political party with the largest number of votes across the four regions would appoint a Prime Minister to form a UK Government in the House of Commons. The next biggest party would elect a Deputy Prime Minister for the UK Government. The Prime Minister and the Deputy Prime Minister would then form a Cabinet from constituency members of the four regional governments in proportion to the number of votes cast for each political party in the regional elections. The political party leaders in the regional governments would supply the UK Prime Minister, with a list of candidates for the Cabinet positions.

This would be a move towards real representative democracy which was described in the book *Evolution to Democracy* by John Creasey, which was published by Hodder and Stoughton in 1969. He said that an 'All Party Alliance' was based on the obvious truth that there are men (and women) of great ability, valuable experience, wisdom and high ideals in every party – and on the firm belief that our system of government should allow the best of all the parties to work together for the good of Britain.

The new UK representative government would produce and present legislation to be debated by the delegates from the four regional parliaments. The legislation will have been prepared by ministers who represent the various political parties, in direct proportion to the votes cast at the general election. This would reduce the adversarial party political debates which currently take place in the Commons chamber.

The consequence of elected regional devolved

governments and an appointed and representative national (UK) government would be to bring the regional constituency members closer to the people they serve and make the national (UK) government more representative of the 'will of the people' as expressed through the voices of regional delegates.

Even if there were no changes to the current arrangements in the House of Commons, we should significantly reduce the number of parliamentary constituencies and the number of Members of Parliament (MPs) from the present 650. This is important so far as the Scottish, Welsh and Northern Irish regions are concerned, as they have regional and national members covering the same ground. We have more political representation in the House of Commons (UK), with 650 elected members, in a country of 63 million people, than they have in the House of Representatives (USA), with 435 elected representatives, in a country of 317 million people.

Whilst we are in the process of reforming the House of Commons, we should turn our attention to the House of Lords. We should dispense with this appointed second chamber of 'hereditary peers' and 'life-peers' and replace it with a mainly elected second chamber. The new chamber could be called the Senate, as in the USA, and counties could elect one or more Senators to represent them in the upper chamber. The present unelected peers could seek election as County Senators but they would be elected as Senators, not appointed as 'Lords of the Realm', which should accord with the prejudice of the 'class conscious' old or New Labour socialists.

Even if there was no fundamental change to the current arrangements, we still need to reduce the number of hereditary and appointed Peers in the House of Lords, which is currently about 800, when they only have 400 seats in the chamber. How can a country of 63 million people justify about 800 non-elected representatives in the

Lords when there are only 100 elected Senators in the USA Senate, a country of 317 million people?

We should also create more independent, transparent and accountable local authorities and town and community or parish councils and bring the local councils and elected councillors much closer to the people they are there to serve. Few citizens actually know the names of their local authority chief executives or directors, who are responsible for the public services which are so important to our local people and communities.

When considering the conflict between the politicians desire to centralise political and economic and taxation powers and the public's desire for the devolution of power, we should consider the following extract from Science Liberty and Peace by Aldous Huxley, published by Chatto and Windus (1947) entitled *Decentralisation of Power*.

"The enormous scientific advantages of the past fifty years have been used primarily to concentrate economic and political power in the hands of a ruling minority and have not been applied to the benefit of society in general. The resulting evils, corruption and despotism among the rulers, the fear and lack of self-reliance among the masses, the spiritual degradation among both, cannot be cured except by wholesale decentralisation."

A socialist Labour Government will always produce a divided society, between Conservatives, whom they allege represent big business and their rich friends and Labour and the trade unions, who claim to be the sole representatives of the working class. Labour socialists also indulge in vindictive attacks on the privileged backgrounds and the public schools attended by some of the Conservative leaders, when many of their own leaders also had a privileged background and attended public schools.

Prior to the last general election (2010) our unelected Prime Minister, Gordon Brown attacked the leader of the Conservative opposition, David Cameron, at Prime Minister's Questions by suggesting that his policies had been 'dreamed up on the playing fields of Eton'. New Labour had embarked on a pre-election campaign, which attacked the privileged lives of their opponents and the new Labour 'offence' of attending a fee-paying public school! They ignored the fact that many of their own socialist ministers, had privileged backgrounds and had attended public schools, which included Alistair Darling 'Loretto'; Jack Straw 'Brentwood'; Ed Balls 'Nottingham High'; Shaun Woodward 'Bristol Grammar'; Harriet Harman 'St Pauls'; Tessa Jowell 'St Margarets' and Tony Blair 'Fettes'.

Don't these socialists understand that 'class warfare' is negative and destructive and should have no part to play in British politics? We need a mature political debate, not the divisive 'politics of envy' and negative 'class warfare' which should be anathema to any grown-up politicians.

Whilst the British electorate, particularly the English, rejected socialism under the guise of Labour at the 2010 General Election and elected a Conservative Liberal Coalition, a call must go out to more conservative minded Liberals to join with more liberal minded Conservatives to form a more permanent alliance, as 93 Liberals did in 1886, a pact which lasted to 1912, when they then formed the Conservative and Unionist Party.

More conservative minded Liberals could have much in common with more liberal minded Conservatives who both would believe in human rights and responsibilities, civil liberties and civic duties and personal freedom and less regulation. They should also have a shared belief in a free-market enterprise economy, fiscal discipline, balanced budgets and 'living within our means'. They should both believe that education is the key to freedom and opportunity and social mobility. They should both believe in the transfer of power from remote institutions to local communities and in particular the reform of the unaccountable European Union. They should also believe that the Welfare State is a safety-net for those in need and that the hallmark of a good society is that vulnerable people are spared from destitution. These many shared beliefs create a very compelling case for an alliance or coalition between the Conservative and Liberal traditions.

Furthermore, more liberal minded fiscal Conservative ministers must reduce the power of the distant European Union (EU) and remote national (and to a lesser extent regional) government and encourage more independent, transparent and accountable local authorities and town and community or parish councils and give more power to the local constituents they are there to serve. This wholesale devolvement of power to the people is the opposite of socialist practice, as in socialist countries the truth is only spoken in the darkness.

It is instructive to note that the founding fathers of the United States of America (USA) wrote the Tenth Amendment to the written Constitution to specifically limit the powers delegated to the federal government. The Tenth Amendment, which is part of the Bill of Rights, ratified on 15 December 1791, was intended to confirm that powers not granted to the Federal Government were reserved for the states or the people, as the founding fathers deeply distrusted government power. It is clear that the Tenth Amendment was written to emphasise the limited nature of the powers delegated to the federal government. When states and local communities take the lead on policy, the people are that much closer to the policy makers and the policy makers are that much closer and more accountable to the people they serve. Adherence to the Tenth Amendment is the first step towards ensuring liberty through decentralisation.

It is also interesting to note, in the context of the extensive powers of the European Union (EU), that the adoption of the Constitution of 1787 was actually opposed by a number of well-known patriots, including Thomas Jefferson, who argued that the Constitution would eventually lead to a strong centralised, state power, which would destroy the individual liberty of the people. Many in this movement were classed as 'Anti-Federalists' and the Tenth Amendment was added to the Constitution because of the intellectual influence and persistence of that movement.

It is the intention of the Conservative Party leadership, under Prime Minister, David Cameron, to renegotiate our relationship with the European Union (EU), should they win the 2015 General Election. He would then let the electorate decide on our continued membership of the European Union in a referendum, planned for 2017. If we are to remain a full member of the European Union, it is essential that we renegotiate the repatriation of legislative powers and stop them increasing their control over member states. A consequence of the proposed negotiations and the prospect of a vote to leave the European Union, is that the Conservatives have been branded 'Euro-Sceptic' by those who favour a federal state, rather than a nationalist approach to governance, which is similar to the attitude towards Thomas Jefferson and the 'Anti-Federalists' in the USA.

Only the Conservatives in government can offer an in-out referendum on our membership of the EU as the Labour Party would only do so for political expediency. The other parties, including UKIP, are unlikely to form a government and cannot, therefore, deliver an in-out referendum.

It is essential that the electorate can differentiate between a more liberal approach to fiscal conservatism and politically adept and economically inept socialism, when it comes to running an enterprise economy. It is only through an efficient private sector that we can create the wealth to finance the growing public demand for more efficient public services.

It is also essential that the electorate can differentiate between a more liberal approach to fiscal conservatism, which would support limited government, and divisive unionised socialism, which supports a big-state. The concept of smaller government and bigger people will only emerge from a more liberal approach to fiscal conservatism and the devolution of economic and taxation powers to the lowest practical level.

It is only when we have persuaded the electorate to adopt a more liberal approach to fiscal conservatism and when we have achieved the devolution of economic and taxation powers to local government that we can turn our attention to the concept of bigger people and a stronger society.

However, we can only achieve a better society, through a process of education for responsible citizenship, more contemporary community policing and inspirational community leadership and the ultimate goal of social improvement, community renewal and real social justice.

CHAPTER 3:

We Need Education for Responsible Citizenship

The road to citizenship passes by the schoolhouse

We live in a society where the critical social values and moral standards of ordinary people are influenced by those responsible for the mass media. We live in a society where citizens elected to public office abuse the privilege of serving the people, creating a climate of public apathy and indifference to the political and electoral process. We live in a society damaged by serious criminal and antisocial behaviour which produces a climate of fear and apprehension. We live in a society where the social divisions between the rich and the poor are increasing rapidly. We live in a society of strangers where civic values and pride have been neglected and a society tainted by bad manners and incivility towards our fellow citizens. We live in an impersonal society dominated by the World Wide Web and the social media revolution, where we have lost the art of personal contact. It is against this background that we must debate the importance of education for citizenship, which is an essential element in the desire for social improvement, community renewal and social justice.

So far as education for citizenship is concerned we should consider the following from *A World is Waiting to be Born: The Search for Civility* by M Scott Peck, published by Random House in 1993, which states why they funded public education in the USA, as follows:

> *"In the early days of the nation there had been great debate over whether there should be public education supported by taxation. The debate was resolved on the grounds that in order to sustain a democratic society, public education was required for the widespread teaching of civics. By civics our leaders meant deep-seated values that would be a foundation for responsible citizenship, necessary to maintain a healthy democracy."*

A more liberal conservative approach to public education would emphasise the importance of vocational training and education for responsible citizenship, as opposed to the New Labour obsession with the majority of young people, particularly from disadvantaged backgrounds, going to university, when university may not be their best option. We must, therefore, emphasise the crucial importance of vocational training and education for responsible citizenship, as we need many more fine young citizens ready for the world of work and community leadership.

The importance of education for citizenship was recognised in *The Population of Britain* by Eva M Hubback, Pelican Books (1947) which said:

> *"How are we to carry out in our schools education for citizenship,*

the most important aspect of which is a sense of social responsibility, when the child's success in life depends on his vocational training. It is (therefore) not surprising that the child's social education has been neglected. (Furthermore) the need to develop a feeling of responsibility for the nation and smaller groups must be stressed in schools. It must be taught in the classroom, gained through contact with fine individuals and practiced in the daily life of the school and in service to the community."

The following quote from *Education* by Lester Smith, published by Penguin Books (1970), under the headings 'The Board of Education's Handbook of Suggestions for Teachers' and 'Education 1900-1950' said:

"This strong emphasis on character training, which began in Public Schools, has become normal throughout our educational system. Character training is linked with the concept of school as a society. We think of pupils growing up and gaining experience of leadership and service. In recent years there has been an emphasis on the need to foster a spirit of service and a sense of responsibility. We think of children, not only as individuals but as citizens growing up and getting accustomed to their duties and responsibilities."

The following extract from *Save the Family, Save the Child* by Vincent J Fontana and Valerie Moolman, published by the Penguin Group (USA) in 1991, had this to say on the responsibilities of our schools and teachers, towards a sense of citizenship:

"Schools can teach, even if parents can't, and even if teachers are weary and discouraged. I call on them to teach what they used to teach, common civility, respect for the rights of others, respect for human life and the quality of life, respect for country, a sense of citizenship, civic pride and personal standards of ethics, what is right

and what is wrong and moral responsibility. Some parents can teach it themselves, others can't because they never learned it themselves. Whether we like it or not, we must play catch-up or the kids will grow up as amoral and ignorant and violent as their parents."

Incidentally, in our desire for the development of a sense of citizenship, a sense of civic pride, a sense of community spirit and a deep feeling of belonging, we may be overlooking a critical social precondition of a sense of nationhood and patriotism. This pride of nationhood and patriotism must not be confused with xenophobia, which means a dislike of foreigners or strangers. We can be proud of our nation, which means the people living and belonging to a single state, a race of people of common descent, a sense of history, a sense of language and a sense of common culture, without having feelings of xenophobia. We can be proud of our culture, which means our customs, our mores of a particular civilisation or society, without disrespecting the culture, the customs and mores of foreigners. We can be proud of our moral and social values without devaluing the moral and social values of others. We can be proud to be patriotic, which means that we are loyal and devoted to our country, without demeaning the feelings of loyalty and devotion of those economic migrants and asylum seekers who come from other parts of the world and still harbour feelings of pride for their original homeland.

However, as we develop as a multi-cultural, multi-racial and multi-faith society, through a process of immigration, inevitably the culture, religion, customs, traditions and values of the host community, will be significantly influenced by the different cultures, religions, customs, traditions and values of the immigrant population. This includes legal or illegal immigrants and genuine or bogus asylum seekers from a multitude of countries suffering human rights violations and military conflicts, which creates a massive displacement problem and no international dispersal or repatriation solutions. This vacuum is filled by criminal gangs who transport refugees to 'wealthy' western European countries, whose public services are stretched to the limit by so many 'asylum seekers' with a multitude of different languages, expecting to be provided with free housing, free health care, free education and welfare benefits to survive.

However, whilst the numbers of refugees are increasing dramatically, this process of integration and assimilation should not be too difficult for an island nation with a history of immigration or invasion. We are a nation of immigrants, from the Celts, Romans, Angles, Saxons, Vikings, Danes, Jutes, Normans, the oppressed Jews and persecuted Huguenots, the Hungarians, Czechoslovakians, Germans, Italians, Polish, Irish and other Northern Europeans. Whilst our history suggests that we are very much a nation of immigrants or invaders, the majority of immigrants were northern Europeans, who had similar cultures, customs, beliefs and skin colour and they managed to integrate without too much difficulty, despite different languages and some resistance to inter-marriage.

More recently due to the 'Blair Wars' in the Balkans, Afghanistan and Iraq we have experienced a massive displacement of (mainly) Muslims to our shores. During the wars in the Balkans (1990s) we are told that hundreds of thousands of Bosnians, Kosovans, Croats and others, mostly Muslims, were displaced and became refugees in Europe. Furthermore, over 150,000 Bosnians were thought to have settled in the UK by 1994.

We probably have no idea how many Muslims from Iraq and Afghanistan and the more recent civil war in Syria have sought refuge in our country and the demands they make on our essential public services and whether they intend to settle permanently or eventually return to their homeland.

There is, however, no doubt that immigration is an

explosive political issue which will dominate the headlines for many years to come and will benefit the United Kingdom Independence Party (UKIP), which exists to leave the European Union. Furthermore, when we discuss the challenges of integration and assimilation of immigrants into our benevolent and tolerant society, we should probably revisit our extensive experiences with the Caribbean, Indian, Pakistan and Bangladesh communities who came to our shores (mainly) in the second half of the 20th Century.

The integration of West Indian immigrants was affected by a different culture, traditions, dialect, skin colour and the psychological effects of the slave trade, together with a feeling of racial discrimination, making integration and assimilation very difficult, even to those born in this country of immigrant parents. We now have a serious social problem of street gangs, gun crimes, knife crimes and illegal drug dealing in our inner-city neighbourhoods, which often involves young black men and seriously damages the fabric of our inner-city neighbourhoods and makes the concept of education for responsible citizenship much more difficult.

It is extremely difficult for our mainly white northern European citizens to make objective social judgements and find enduring social solutions to the complex social problems of black youth behaviour. Consequently, if we hope to integrate our often disenfranchised young black men into our mainly white British society and constructively engage them in a process of education for responsible citizenship, we must carefully listen to the views of prominent black citizens from black communities. However, the biggest challenge in the black Caribbean communities is the phenomenon of 'absent fathers' and the adverse effect it has on the social behaviour of young black men, being raised in single parent, low-income households.

More recently, Asian immigrants from India, both Hindu and Muslim, and from Pakistan and Bangladesh, mainly Muslim, present different challenges to integration and assimilation, due to different cultures, customs, traditions and religious beliefs. In the case of a minority of vociferous Muslims, they practice Islamic fundamentalism and threaten death to non-believers or infidels, which is the majority of the tolerant and benevolent host community! What happened to the principle 'When in Rome, do as the Romans do' and what happened to respect for the culture, customs, traditions and religions of the host community?

So far as education for responsible citizenship is concerned and the ability of the immigrant community to integrate and assimilate into our society, which is essential for social harmony, the Muslim immigrant community, who practice the Islamic faith, are against marriage outside of their religion and their elders prefer arranged marriages, both of which damage social integration and assimilation. Furthermore, some Muslim women wear the Niqab or Burka, a full-face covering with a gap for the eyes, which must affect their ability to communicate and socialise and integrate. Muslims also conform to 'theocratic' Sharia Law, which is the law of God, the body of religious doctrines that regulate their lives, which reduces the importance of democracy and man-made laws. For these reasons, the strict adherence of Muslim immigrants to Islam is bound to slow down social integration and assimilation into a mainly Christian or secular society and a liberal western democracy and make the concept of education for citizenship more difficult to achieve.

However, the practice of wearing the veil should not be an issue in a liberal permissive society, as many indigenous women used to wear a headscarf many years ago. The main issue is with the practice of wearing a full-face covering in public places and public buildings, which is bound to be a barrier to social integration and does have some security issues. However, just banning the Niqab and Burka, rather than any full-face covering in public places, would be seen as discrimination by the Muslim faith community and would raise complex law enforcement issues. The French Government had the courage to ban full-face coverings in public places and have been challenged by many Muslim women who believe it is their human right to wear full-face covers in public places, based upon their religious beliefs. The British Government, however, has said that it is not for governments to decide what people should wear in the street.

Whilst the indigenous Christian or secular host community may have strong views about the wearing of the Niqab or Burka in public places, as a barrier to integration and assimilation, which Islamic fundamentalists would consider to be religious intolerance by the host community, it is more appropriate to consider the views of Britain's first Muslim Peer, Lord Ahmed. He was reported in The Times, 21 February 2007, to condemn the wearing of the Niqab (which was originally introduced to protect vulnerable women from harassment by dominant men) as a 'physical barrier to integration' when he said:

"The veil (the niqab) is now (seen as) a mark of separation, segregation and defiance against mainstream British culture (and) there's nothing in the Koran to say that the wearing of the Niqab is desirable, let alone compulsory."

Reasonable men and women from the host community would sympathise with Muslim elders concerned for the spiritual wellbeing of their young women who are encouraged to integrate into a permissive western liberal society, which suffers the abuse of alcohol, the illegal drugs epidemic and a promiscuous sexual revolution. However, we need to develop mutual respect between the host community's desire for the social integration of immigrant women and the immigrant communities desire to protect their women from the adverse effects of a permissive western liberal society.

To show the extent of the challenge to integrate our diverse cultural, racial and faith communities, towards common citizenship, with the many different cultures, customs, traditions and values of the immigrant and indigenous population, the following are the numbers of different nationalities resident in our country as recorded by an IPPR census in 2001; India 466,416; Pakistan 320,767; Bangladesh 154,201; Caribbean 254,740; Kenya 129,356; Nigeria 88,105; Sri Lanka 67,832; Turkey 53,964; Cyprus 77,156; South Africa 140,201; Spain 54,105; Hong Kong 94,611; Germany 262,276; USA 155,030; Italy 107,002; Australia 106,404; France 94,178; Canada 70,145 and New Zealand 57,916.

Then we have hundreds of thousands of economic migrants from the eight former Soviet Union bloc countries which joined the European Union in 2004, that's Poland, the Czech Republic, Slovakia, Hungary, Estonia, Lithuania, Latvia and Slovenia, together with Malta and Cyprus. Then we have many immigrants from Bulgaria and Romania (Moldova) which joined the EU in 2007 and Croatia which joined the EU in 2013 and many others from the adjacent former communist countries. Then we have thousands of asylum seekers, often supported by criminal gangs, from the war-torn countries of North Africa, such as Somalia and Sudan and the Middle East, such as Afghanistan, Iraq, Syria and Palestine.

More recent information from the Office for National Statistics (ONS), released in February 2009, showed that 6.5 million people resident in Britain in the year to June 2008, were born overseas, a rise of 1.2 million since 2004, and about 11% of the population of the United Kingdom. They included residents born in India 619,000, Poland 461,000, Ireland 416,000, Pakistan 415,000, Germany 265,000, South Africa 203,000, Bangladesh 189,000, United States of America 180,000, Jamaica 164,000 and Nigeria 139,000 besides the many thousands of illegal immigrants.

We were also recently told by the United Nations that the world has 50 million displaced persons and asylum seekers fleeing persecution and poverty and there are no global distribution solutions to integrate and assimilate such large numbers into those countries which are free from conflict and capable of absorbing such large population displacement.

If ever we had a challenge of integration and assimilation of citizenship in this complex multi-cultural, multi-racial and multi-faith society, the present rate of immigration, both legal and illegal, is unprecedented and unsustainable and even the language differences place an intolerable burden on our public services, such as health and education and police.

It was recently suggested that the former New Labour government, which had lost control of immigration, had been practicing a form of social engineering, without the approval of the electorate, to change our society by mass immigration, creating a more multi-cultural, multi-racial and multi-faith society. They no doubt believed that many immigrants from Eastern Europe and many asylum seekers from the war-torn countries of the Middle East and North Africa would be unfamiliar with liberalism or conservatism and more familiar with socialism, which would be to their electoral advantage. It would, of course, be gross negligence for them to let immigration run out of control, regardless of the increased pressures on communities and public services, just to achieve electoral advantage.

Nevertheless, we must continue to promote the positive aspects of a multi-cultural, multi-racial and multi-faith society, we must highlight the many social benefits of cultural, racial and religious diversity and we must oppose cultural and racial discrimination and religious intolerance.

Furthermore, if the pride of nationhood and patriotism is an important part of education for British citizenship and the culture, customs and traditions of the indigenous population are being eroded by the process of immigration, with immigrants who have a pride of nationhood and patriotism for a foreign country, the land of their forebears, the process of education for British citizenship will be much more challenging.

Despite difficulties in defining a process of education for citizenship, due to the protracted process of immigration and the diversity of nationhood and patriotism and their cultures and customs, we must develop a process which is based on a celebration of the differences which are endemic in a rich, multi-cultural, multi-racial and multi-faith society, in the certain knowledge that racial, cultural and religious differences will be reduced through the natural process of inter-marriage and the increasing use of the host nation language and the acceptance of each other's religions.

However, whilst racial, cultural and religious harmony is essential to achieve a programme of education for British citizenship, how do those who adhere to a strict Islamic religion and believe in theocracy, integrate into a secular liberal western democracy? How can an Islamic culture, which opposes inter-marriage and favours polygamy, integrate with a Christian religion, which believes in the freedom of inter-marriage and the restriction of monogamy?

Furthermore, how do we achieve social integration and assimilation, when some British Muslim clerics have openly preached death to infidels or non-believers, which effectively means death to the majority of the host community, who do not practice the Islamic faith? We have also suffered the devastating consequences of extreme violence caused by some Muslim fundamentalists who have been indoctrinated to become suicide bombers.

We must now hear the voices of moderate Muslim leaders, who disagree with extreme violence in the name of Islam, which is a name derived from the word 'Salam', an Arabic word for peace. World leaders and religious leaders must help the Muslim community to establish an international leadership organisation, similar to other religions, such as Catholicism, which can speak for the Islamic religion throughout the world. Sadly, the present vacuum, which exists in Islamic leadership throughout the world, has been filled by Islamic fundamentalists who are prepared to impose their extreme religious views onto the world through extreme violence.

Sadiq Khan, a New Labour minister and a Muslim was reported on Sky News, 17 September 2008, to have accused British Muslims of having a victim mentality and he listed a number of issues they need to address to enable them to integrate, including:

"Mosques should consider allowing women in and should tackle sexism; Muslims who don't speak English should learn English; Muslims should condemn forced marriages and honour killings and that a failure to deal with the inequalities of British Muslim women flies in the face of attempts to build a socially just and fair society and … we need to leave behind our victim mentality."

Dilwar Hussain, a senior Islamic scholar from the Islamic Foundation, in a recent essay for the Institute for Public Policy Research, argued for the evolution of a new brand of Islam, which was tailored to living conditions in Britain. He said that the new theology of Islam would have to address the inequality of women in some misogynistic

Muslim cultures. He also said that Muslims had failed to do enough to challenge extremists and promoters of terrorism and that they had done too little to produce leaders who can educate young people and guide them away from extremism. He promoted the idea that there was a need for Islam, which developed its ideas in countries where Muslims were a majority, to adapt to living as a religious minority in a secular country, with other religions.

We believe that the resistance to Muslim integration into our tolerant and secular liberal western democracy can only be overcome by enlightened Muslim religious community leaders who must persuade their fellow Muslims to show respect for the culture and traditions and religious faith of their benevolent host community. They must also address the obdurate resistance to the natural process of inter-marriage and encourage wider use of the host language and greater participation of women in a secular educational system which is the foundation for success in the workplace.

It is a social imperative that our educational system produces outstanding young men and women, from both the host and immigrant communities, who can compete within the global economy and create the wealth which is necessary for the maintenance of government organisations, essential public services and welfare provision. However, it is of equal importance that we produce fine young citizens, with moral and social values, a sense of responsible citizenship, civic pride, community spirit and social justice.

We must also promote the importance of moral education, character training, socialisation training, education for citizenship and sporting excellence, as examination subjects of equal importance to academic and vocational subjects. Rigid conformance to government imposed national curriculums which are dominated by academic and vocational subjects may ignore the immense social benefits of moral education, character training, socialisation training, education for British citizenship, sporting excellence and a deep sense of civic pride and social responsibilities.

The more that our impressionable children and young people work together in a secular educational environment, regardless of their different social backgrounds, the more they will break down the barriers to integration, as the road to citizenship passes by the schoolhouse.

We must also encourage our developing children and young people against the casual use of obscene and degrading language, which has a debilitating effect upon community wellbeing. However, before we do so the government must put an end to the casual and gratuitous use of obscene and degrading language on our televisions. If it's acceptable on our television screens, it's inevitable in our schools and neighbourhoods.

A more liberal conservative approach to governance should legislate against disgusting, obscene and degrading language, being broadcast into our homes by the television authorities, particularly the British Broadcasting Corporation (BBC), which is responsible to government ministers and financed by public subscription.

We must encourage our children and young people against inconsiderate rudeness and bad manners and encourage a social culture of politeness and good manners. We must encourage our children and young people against the use of aggression and violence towards their fellow citizens, which is often directed against the most vulnerable members of society and leads to a climate of fear and takes us down the slippery slope to bullying, which must be seen as socially and morally reprehensible.

We must also encourage our impressionable children

and young people to develop a sense of civic pride, a sense of community spirit, a sense of social responsibility and a sense of public duty towards their city, their town, their village and their street or neighbourhood. Their elders should, therefore, create an environment which would enable them to develop a sense of pride for their community, their community schools, their community centres and their inspirational community leaders and social entrepreneurs and benevolent philanthropists. It is also important that the mature people in the local community demonstrate leadership by example and recognise and reward the many talented young people who are present in all communities, if we take the bother to recognise them.

Furthermore, government ministers, members of parliament and local councillors, those who we elect to lead us towards a better place, have a public duty to demonstrate inspirational political leadership. However, recent evidence suggests that they cannot maintain acceptable standards of probity and rectitude in the conduct of their political and private lives and ordinary citizens are now cynical about self-serving politicians.

So far as those who indulge in criminal and antisocial behaviour are concerned, often against their own communities, we should consider the withdrawal of some of the benefits of citizenship, pending the acceptance and completion of a rehabilitation process. Welfare benefits must be a short-term safety net to enable those unemployable criminals to find work in community service or voluntary service or charity work. As a caring society, we are too tolerant with persistent and violent criminals, who have no motivation to reform and no motivation to work for their money.

Welfare benefits must not be a career choice for the work-shy, which often leads to incapacity benefits, for those who are able to work but choose to stay at home. Hard choices must be made by egalitarian socialist governments, which have a tendency to support the work-shy, with a cheque in the post and free to work on the black market or lead a life of crime, rather than a series of stepping stones to employment.

Wouldn't it be reasonable for governments of any political persuasion, to ensure that those able-bodied citizens, who have no motivation to work and are unable to hold down regular employment, should be given some form of community or voluntary work, in return for benefits? However, to add insult to injury, to give long-term social security benefits to work-shy people who then indulge in criminal and antisocial behaviour is taking citizens rights too far. Talk about biting the hand that feeds you.

When New Labour came to power in 1997 they promised to deal with the abuse of the welfare system and appointed a Minister for Welfare Reform, who was told to 'think the unthinkable' but he was quickly removed from office and they reverted to type and widespread welfare abuse continued unabated. Realising the level of public concern about welfare abuse, ten years into office, in an attempt to recover their reputation, just prior to an election, they again promised to be tough on benefit cheats but it was too late for any constructive action, it was the usual ministerial distraction!

It's easy for governments to accept people onto welfare programmes but it's very difficult to wean them off dependency and a cheque in the post and free to work on the black market and pay no personal taxation. We hear of whole generations of families who have never worked and exist on welfare hand-outs, with no fear of it being withdrawn, as governments are reliable paymasters to the unproductive section of our society.

There should be no question that any able-bodied

person who is in receipt of long-term unemployment welfare benefits should be seeking work or be provided with work in return for benefits. No able-bodied unemployed person should be supported with a cheque in the post and free to stay at home or work on the black market. Even if they can't or won't find work or are unemployable they should be made to undertake some work, even in the voluntary sector, in return for welfare benefits.

However, the hope that the long-term unemployed will be able to move from generous social housing and welfare benefits into paid employment is unrealistic. It suggests that government policy must be to prevent long-term unemployment by early intervention and the provision of work in the public or voluntary or charity sectors, in return for social benefits.

Young single people, between 18 and 21, who leave full-time education and can't find employment, should be provided with work experience, probably in the form of government sponsored apprenticeships, and should not normally have access to housing benefits when they could live with their family. No young person should have to start their adult lives wholly dependent on state hand-outs and depressing unemployment.

Furthermore, the responsibility to provide education for responsible citizenship in our multi-cultural, multi-ethnic and multi-faith society must start with the extended family. We must discourage the breakdown of families and absent fathers, reinforced by social security advantages. We must encourage the extended family, rather than the state, to accept responsibility for their domestic challenges, when the father is absent.

Whilst it doesn't accord with contemporary thinking, the traditional two parent family - that's a mother and a father, living in the same house, with at least one of them working, rather than on long-term benefits - must be the best environment for children's development. We must also find new ways for mature members of the community to support dysfunctional or disadvantaged families and raise their spirits. In Africa, the saying goes, 'It takes a whole village to raise a child,' and it should be the same here.

This is a great opportunity for the older people in our local communities to show community leadership and encourage responsible citizenship so far as our children and young people are concerned. The older people in our communities often have a wealth of experience and expertise which can be used to support our children and young people. Every village or neighbourhood should have a community support club, which enables the older people to support the younger people through the many community groups, such as the junior schools, the sports clubs and the youth clubs.

We should probably consider the African experience, so far as education for responsible citizenship is concerned. If in Africa, it does take a whole village to raise a child, it must be based on adult authority and mutual respect. Whilst in this country education for responsible citizenship starts in the homes and moves through the schools, it should also involve local communities. Cohesive local communities, which are based on mutual respect and adult authority, should produce more rounded young people who are directed to the road of enterprise and employment, rather than the road to antisocial and criminal behaviour, the courts and the prisons.

CHAPTER 4:

We Need Contemporary Community Policing

Policing with public consent is a proud tradition of the British Police Service

Whilst the solution to the problems of our broken society will involve many complex social factors, a critical factor will be the prevention of criminal and antisocial behaviour on our streets and neighbourhoods. This can only be achieved by an increase in the number of inspirational police officers, walking the streets, leading by the power of example and not by the example of power. Their primary duty would be to work with natural community leaders to prevent nuisance and antisocial behaviour and divert vulnerable children and young people from the path to more serious criminal behaviour and the road to the courts and the prisons.

However, effective community policing will not come from a police service bogged down with too many regulations, too much paperwork and red tape, which removes officers from the streets and confines them to the station. Neither will it come from a reactive service, overwhelmed by the repetitive cycle of criminal and antisocial behaviour. Neither will it come from cynical officers, working within a criminal justice system which favours community service orders and probation orders for many persistent criminals, with no motivation to reform. Neither will it come from weary officers with a siege mentality, operating in a hostile social environment, with limited resources chasing unlimited public demand and unrealistic public expectations. It will only come from a more contemporary approach to community policing, where inspirational officers with community leadership experience, walk the streets and neighbourhoods and become community organisers and community activists and problem solvers, to create safe and secure communities.

There must be a transition from reactive policing, which responds to antisocial and criminal behaviour, to more proactive policing, which is concerned with diverting young people from nuisance, antisocial and criminal behaviour. This transition will need additional resources to divert the young people and reduce their bad behaviour and a subsequent reduction in resources when the prevention and diversion programme has achieved its objectives and the need to respond to incidents is reduced.

We live in a society where the public perception is that criminal and antisocial behaviour got worse during the tenure of the former socialist government and that many people were afraid to walk the streets at night. Many streets in urban areas had been taken over by young hooligans and had been abandoned by the police. However, New Labour insisted that they had increased investment into the police service and had increased the numbers of police officers and that the crime rate was either coming down or the rate of increase was slowing down but what was the truth?

Research by the United Nations Regional Information Centre into comparative crime levels in the European Union (EU) entitled *The Burden of Crime in the EU* (2007) claimed that Britain was a 'high crime rate' country. The research said that although the rates for some offences, such as property and vehicle crime, may have declined, largely because of more sophisticated security, the incidence of assault and threats of personal violence had risen inexorably since the 1990s, in contrast to most other EU countries where crime rates had generally fallen. Britain had the highest level of burglary in 2004 of any of the eighteen countries surveyed. Remarkably, they found no association between levels of crime and poverty or even economic inequality but the abuse of alcohol is the one feature which is linked with rising crime.

To make matters worse the Chief Inspector of Prisons reported in October 2007 that we had 11,000 foreign nationals in our prisons. This means that our police officers, who appear to have vacated the streets, where they would have been protecting the law-abiding citizens, have been occupied with foreign national criminals, many of whom have no legitimate reason to be in our country. When we consider the wide range of nationalities and foreign languages spoken by these criminals, we can imagine the burden they imposed on the police service the courts and the prisons. The 11,000 foreign prisoners included 1,464 from Jamaica, 1,061 from Nigeria, 653 from Ireland, 419 from Pakistan, 406 from Vietnam, 356 from Somalia, 315 from India, 312 from China, 312 from Poland, 264 from Iraq, 225 from Turkey, 210 from South Africa, 207 from Ghana, 194 from Iran, 194 from Zimbabwe, 193 from Algeria, 191 from Lithuania, 183 from Portugal, 170 from France, 169 from Sri Lanka, 167 from Bangladesh, 150 from Romania, 148 from Albania,

132 from the Netherlands, 129 from Germany, 124 from Columbia, 113 from Russia, 111 from the Congo, 106 from Italy and 103 from the USA.

Being part of the European Union (EU) means that millions of citizens from the many member states are free to travel and settle and work in this country, whether they can speak our language, whether there are homes available, whether there is any work and whether our public services can cope, yet some are prepared to abuse our hospitality with antisocial and criminal behaviour. Furthermore, many foreign nationals from war-torn countries or countries with poor human rights records seek asylum in our benevolent country, often assisted by illegal 'human traffic' gangs, and our compassion is rewarded with antisocial and criminal behaviour.

How can any police service cope with foreign criminals from so many different countries, who speak so many different languages and are not known to the authorities? Furthermore, how can they cope with so many foreign criminals, from so many different countries, when they have no immediate access to their computerised criminal records or their vehicle registration and insurance records, as they have in this country?

The free movement of criminals throughout the European Union is a serious problem for any police service, which is rendered ineffective in the absence of computerised criminal records and vehicle registration records. It is made worse by the fact that police officers in the various countries of the European Union are not aware of the movements of these criminals across uncontrolled borders and when they come across them, often in foreign registered vehicles, they may have no idea who they are.

Had there not been so many foreign criminals in our prisons, during the tenure of the New Labour government, they would not have had an over-crowding problem and would not have had to authorise an early release programme, to free up prison places, and we would not have had our own criminals back on the streets, continuing their lives of crime. If there were not so many foreign criminals in our country, taking advantage of our liberal democracy, the police service would be able to spend more time on the streets dealing with the damage caused by our own criminals.

Social justice will only be served by dedicated community police officers, working with natural community leaders, building a climate of mutual respect and policing with the consent and support of the public. This is much more preferable than a remote mobile 'hit and run' response to incidents of antisocial and criminal behaviour. The essence of 'policing with the consent of the public' is that police officers must be seen as part of the local community and trusted by the local people, rather than being seen as detached, impersonal and remote outsiders.

Community policing must be the primary response to antisocial and criminal behaviour in our communities and must not be a secondary response to what is known as 'Fire Brigade' policing. Furthermore, community policing must be run by dedicated police officers with a social conscience and a personal mission. This is certainly not a soft option for officers looking for a quiet life. How can the police service change from an impersonal emergency response system, where police officers in cars respond to a hostile social environment, to a proactive system, where antisocial and criminal behaviour is defused at source by dedicated community police officers, walking the streets and neighbourhoods?

This is a cost-effective form of community policing, where mature community constables, supported by community support officers, could manage a number of communities or neighbourhoods, harnessing the energy of volunteer special constables and street co-ordinators and policing with the consent of the public. To cover the ground with mature community constables is an opportunity for the authorities to re-employ retired police officers, on short term contracts, who would otherwise be lost to the service. The retention of these experienced police officers, as dedicated community constables, working alongside natural community leaders, would reduce any recruitment, training and inexperience costs, making this approach to community policing very cost-effective.

The traditional role of a community constable, under the management of more senior police officers, is much more than a law enforcement agent and their main duties must be crime prevention, reduction and diversion. They must also have impressive leadership qualities and be seen as role models and mentors to our vulnerable children and impressionable young people. They must be free to demonstrate community leadership qualities and be catalysts for crime prevention, crime reduction and the diversion of our young people from the road to antisocial and criminal behaviour.

So what are the arguments to support an increase in the number of real community police officers, as opposed to community support officers? In the first instance the British police service is known as one of the best law enforcement agencies in the world. Their recruitment standards attract people with impressive educational standards. The probationary period of two years removes those who fail to achieve the required standards. Training programmes ensure high standards of legal knowledge and police procedures which are essential to deal with the adversarial criminal justice system and an increasingly litigious society. The promotion system, which includes legal examinations and personal assessments, ensures high standards of supervision and management. The discipline code and the public complaints system ensure the maintenance of high standards of service delivery and the command training provides a continuous source of chief officers capable of inspirational leadership.

With that level of professional experience, developed in a public service environment, why would any government want mature police officers to retire from the service then have to recruit and train and manage their replacements? Furthermore, many experienced operational officers are frustrated with the increasing bureaucracy in the criminal justice system and the socialist nonsense of imposing arbitrary targets and performance measurements, which destroys their initiative and discretion, which is the hallmark of the 'bobby on the beat', and they often can't wait to retire.

Whilst there will continue to be public debate about the funding of the police service and the role of community support officers, who were introduced by New Labour and offer a cheaper alternative to regular police officers, the most effective method of community policing must involve trained community constables, with the authority to deal with antisocial and criminal behaviour in our many troubled communities.

However, we must not diminish the personal courage of community support officers, who wear the uniform and walk the streets and confront antisocial and criminal behaviour in support of the regular police and on behalf of law-abiding citizens. Nevertheless, the authorities should increase the training of community support officers and where possible elevate them to community constables and phase out the role completely.

Whilst we can probably have three community support officers for two community constables, the community would probably prefer the latter.

We live in a society concerned with social improvement, community renewal and social justice, which needs a proactive crime prevention service working with local communities, rather than a reactive mobile emergency response service, with no affinity with ordinary citizens. If police officers spend too much time in the station or in their patrol cars, rather than walking the streets, they will lose public contact and public support, which is an essential ingredient of 'policing with the consent of the public', which is an essential element of a democratic police service.

We must return to the respected 'bobby on the beat' in accordance with the *raison d'etre* of the original police service, which was defined by a Parliamentary Select Committee, chaired by Member of Parliament and Home Secretary, Robert Peel in 1822 as follows:

"A system of regular patrolling of the streets of the capital should be established to reduce crime and disorder. The recommendation of a patrol consists of its tendency to harass and banish the offender by preserving an 'annoying scrutiny' and preventing the commission of crime and disorder."

The introduction of community support officers by the former New Labour government, as a cheap alternative to street police officers, has made fully trained officers 'strangers to the streets' and made walking the streets below their 'pay grade'. Worse still, it has made many police officers 'elitist', not to be confused with lesser trained community support officers. However, insulting brave community support officers as a cheap alternative to regular officers, who are now confined to their cars, is a contradiction in terms. They are the ones who walk the streets and are first at the scene of incidents. They are in the front line and should be respected for their bravery, not ridiculed for not being 'proper bobbies'.

It's probably not unreasonable to observe that the

increase in violence and antisocial behaviour on our streets and neighbourhoods coincided with the vacation of our streets and neighbourhoods by police officers. Sadly, they have left ordinary members of the public to protect themselves and their families against violence and aggression on our streets and neighbourhoods and suffer the consequences should they go too far.

New Labour ministers damaged the effectiveness and efficiency of the police service by creating too much legislation and too many regulations and too much bureaucracy, making the job of catching criminals and taking them before the criminal courts just too difficult. They created an army of desk-bound officers, wrestling with the increasing administrative demands of the criminal justice system in general and the bureaucratic Crown Prosecution Service in particular. They should have released the officers from unnecessary paperwork and returned them to the streets and neighbourhoods, working with natural community leaders, to prevent and deter antisocial and criminal behaviour, before it got out of control.

Increased bureaucracy drags operational police officers off the streets, into the safety of the police stations, abandoning the streets to those who indulge in criminal and antisocial behaviour and abandoning the law-abiding majority to defend themselves and risk arrest and prosecution if they go too far. The long list of ordinary decent law-abiding citizens who have been killed or seriously injured, when confronting violent young people on our streets, and the arrest and prosecution of others thought to have gone too far, in defence of their homes and families, is a travesty of justice by the Crown Prosecution Service and the criminal justice system.

If we had sufficient dedicated community constables on our streets and neighbourhoods, who could prevent criminal and antisocial behaviour and give the public a feeling of security and safety, then they wouldn't have to attempt to protect themselves and their families from persistent violent criminals, who are a law unto themselves. Why did New Labour ministers, who stormed to power with the mantra 'tough on crime, tough on the causes of crime', fail to increase the number of real community constables, rather than community support officers, during a period of unprecedented economic success? Real community constables have the legal authority and the strength of character to reclaim our streets from those who indulge in criminal and antisocial behaviour, which is what the general public should be able to expect from their police service.

Perhaps government ministers and members of parliament of any political persuasion should revisit the clause in The Metropolitan Police Act 1829, which emphasised the importance of crime prevention rather than crime detection, as follows:

"To this great end, the prevention of crime, every effort of the police is to be directed. The security of persons and property, the preservation of public tranquillity, will thus be better affected than by the detection and punishment of the offender, after he has succeeded in committing the crime."

We need an increase in dedicated community constables, rather than community support officers, walking the streets and neighbourhoods of our cities, towns and villages, to deter and prevent and reduce criminal and antisocial behaviour, working with concerned citizens. There must also be a complete overhaul of the bureaucratic criminal justice system to concentrate limited resources on reducing violent criminal and antisocial behaviour and providing real support to the neglected victims of crime.

Whilst this may seem elementary, we must have a

system, throughout the service, of targeting persistent criminals and disqualified drivers. Every operational officer should have a duty to supervise a number of persistent criminals and disqualified drivers and gather information/intelligence about their nefarious activities and design a proactive response to deter or reduce their criminal behaviour or their driving whilst disqualified, rather than prosecuting them and leaving them without supervision.

Furthermore, if persistent criminals, such as burglars, were imprisoned at the earliest opportunity in their criminal careers, rather than making excuses for their behaviour and giving them non-custodial sentences, the number of burglaries would reduce dramatically, as some burglars are literally 'one man crime waves'. This would give the police service and the public some long-overdue respite from repetitive crimes and ensure that more officers are available for street patrol. Locking up persistent criminals, with no motivation to reform, rather than giving them non-custodial sentences, would be great value for money. Such a policy would, of course, be resisted by 'bleeding heart' liberals who would be concerned about their human rights, rather than those of their victims.

Those who support non-custodial sentences for persistent criminals with no motivation to reform, particularly probation orders, should consider the words of Peter Coad, a former senior probation officer and director of the Criminal Justice Association, who was reported as saying at the start of the millennium:

"We believe Britain's high crime rate is due to community-based sentences given to persistent criminals with no initiative to reform. We estimate the crime rate could be cut by a third within two years if non-custodial sentences were given to those who genuinely want to break

*their crime habit. Probation is not protecting the public from crime.
To do so persistent offenders must be jailed."*

The following extract from a document produced by
the National Probation Directorate (NPD) in 2006 and
circulated to senior probation officers, destroys the
argument for probation orders for persistent and recidivist
and habitual criminals with no motivation to reform:

*"More than 10,000 crimes a month are committed by offenders
on probation. An average of 7,800 criminals are arrested, cautioned
or convicted each month while under the supervision of the Probation
Service. They are responsible for 10,206 offences a month, ranging
from theft and assault to rape and murder."*

It is, however, just common sense to appreciate that
persistent criminals, on probation orders, probably commit
many more crimes than the ones for which they are
arrested, cautioned or convicted.

So far as the prosecution of minor criminal matters is
concerned, we must reduce the bureaucracy in the Crown
Prosecution Service and defence solicitor created delays in
the court process and the cost of dealing with minor
matters. Those arrested for minor public order offences
should be quickly charged and taken before a sitting
magistrate, where the criminal would enter a guilty plea,
the evidence would be summarised, a 'duty solicitor' would
give mitigating circumstances and the magistrates would
give a lenient, non-custodial, sentence. This simple system
of instant justice would cut out increased bureaucracy and
unnecessary delays in the court process, caused by the
demands of defence solicitors, reducing police paperwork
and getting operational officers back onto the streets.

So far as the massive foreign prison population is

concerned, whether they are economic migrants from other member states of the European Union or elsewhere in the world or whether they are genuine or dubious asylum seekers or just visitors who have overstayed their welcome, they have abused their right to stay in our benevolent and tolerant country.

Government ministers must protect our law-abiding citizens from these dangerous foreign criminals and deport them back to their countries of origin on their release from prison but what are the rules about the deportation of serious foreign criminals from the EU and elsewhere?

Any non-British citizens can be deported for a variety of reasons but unless a court has recommended deportation, it's unusual for the Home Secretary to initiate deportation, unless there is an overwhelming public need. There is, however, a distinction between the EU citizens and other foreign nationals. If a prison sentence for an EU citizen was more than two years or other foreign nationals more than one year they can be deported. A foreign national may be made the subject of a deportation order when the Home Secretary believes that it is in the interests of the public good or when he or she is the spouse, civil partner or child of someone subject of a deportation order or where he or she is over 17 years old and has been convicted of a criminal offence which carries with it a prison sentence and the court recommended that he be deported once he has served his sentence. In January 2015 there were 4,247 foreign criminals living in Britain and awaiting deportation and 758 of them, including murderers, rapists, robbers and paedophiles had vanished.

According to the Home Office a record number of foreign criminals won appeals against deportation on human rights grounds in 2012/13. There were 602 appeals allowed, which included 324 criminals who won the right to stay in Britain under the controversial 'Right to Private and Family Life', set out in Article 8 of the European Convention on Human Rights'. The total number of appeals included 113 offenders who were convicted of serious or violent offences, including murder, manslaughter, rape, indecent assault and child sexual abuse. Three foreign criminals, who had been convicted of murder or manslaughter, actually won their appeals against deportation from Britain on human rights grounds. We must question why these dangerous foreign criminals and their families can't have a 'Right to Private and Family Life' in their own country.

To put the problem of foreign criminals into perspective, the following numbers of Europeans convicted in Britain in 2010 were as follows; Poland 6,777; Romania 4,343; Lithuania 4,170; Ireland 2,423; Latvia 1,938; Portugal 1,842; France 1,032; Czech Republic 783; Italy 706; Netherlands 516; Slovakia 361; Germany 360; Spain 267; Bulgaria 296; Hungary 290; Estonia 181; Cyprus 162; Sweden 104; Greece 102; Malta 70; Denmark 61; Austria 58; Finland 58; Slovenia 24; Belgium 23; Luxembourg 3; Total 27,056. The question is how many of these were recommended for deportation by the Home Secretary or a court of law?

However, so far as our home-grown criminals are concerned, besides the additional problem of foreign criminals, the evidence suggests that the police and the courts alone are unable to stem the tide. They clearly need the willing support of families and friends and local communities to deal with minor incidents of criminal and antisocial behaviour before it moves from the homes, to the schools, to the streets and the courts and prisons, which should be a last resort.

It would also be interesting to develop a system of 'community hearings' run by community or parish councils and councillors and well respected community leaders, which would consider minor incidents of nuisance, antisocial and criminal behaviour by local children and young people. Their parents or teachers or councillors would be able to take them to a 'community hearing' and they would be held accountable to their local community for their bad behaviour. They would be given a 'community warning' or 'community work' in response to their antisocial behaviour. If the parents or their children and teenagers refuse to accept a decision of a 'community hearing', they would then be referred to the police and criminal courts. These 'community hearings' would serve to define the relationship between the children and young people and the community.

Furthermore, every community should have a 'community support club', which would support community groups, particularly those involving the children and young people. The main purpose of a 'community support club' would be for older people to support younger people, through local community groups, such as primary and junior schools, sports clubs and youth clubs. They would also support disadvantaged young people and those who have strayed into nuisance and antisocial behaviour, to divert them from the road to the courts and the prisons. The older people could also use their extensive work experience to mentor the young people and ensure that they are ready for the world of work. Where our young people have strayed into criminal and antisocial behaviour, could it be in direct proportion to a lack of community leadership from the older citizens?

The approach of any conservative government to the break-down of law and order on our streets and neighbourhoods should involve an increase in real community constables, community support officers and volunteer special constables, who would co-ordinate social action from the streets. They would work as community leaders and organisers and activists and work with local authority services and the voluntary sector in an attempt to divert young people from nuisance, antisocial and criminal behaviour.

This process of community leadership from the streets would reduce the future need to arrest, charge, prosecute and incarcerate young offenders. It would also reduce the workload of the police service, the prosecuting authorities, the criminal courts, the probation service and then reduce the prison population and the adverse effects of these 'universities of crime'.

For those recidivist criminals, caught up in a perpetual cycle of crime and incarceration with no motivation to reform a more conservative approach would increase the public resources available to rehabilitation, to ensure that they are given greater support to break their repetitive cycle of crime. They could also be given community work, to earn their social benefits and get work experience when they leave incarceration, rather than a cheque in the post and free to roam. However, any attempt to make the unemployed or the unemployable earn their social benefits through community work, will meet with resistance from liberal minded people, who see social benefits as an 'entitlement' and the thought of working for social benefits or entitlements as a form of 'slave labour'!

Furthermore, the world would be a much better place if the majority of our prisons were modern 'state of the art' rehabilitation centres, which concentrated resources on the rehabilitation of persistent criminals. We would still need some traditional prisons to house persistent and violent criminals, with no motivation to reform, who must be locked up to protect the public. Whilst prisons are thought to be counter-productive, on the basis that they 'come out worse than they went in', they would always be able to transfer to modern 'state of the art' rehabilitation centres, should they wish to mend their criminal ways and return to main stream society.

No one should be released from incarceration, except through a modern rehabilitation centre, and no one should be released from a rehabilitation centre to survive on social security dependence, illegal drug dependence, alcohol abuse and criminal and antisocial behaviour. As they move from the security of incarceration to the insecurity of the streets, they will need continued support. However, their reliance on state benefits, while they continue their criminal and antisocial behaviour, effectively 'biting the hand that feeds them', cannot be tolerated, even under a more liberal conservative approach to criminal justice. Those who are thought to be unemployable must be given community or voluntary or charitable work in return for welfare benefits, which would give them the dignity of work experience and less time on their hands for other less productive things.

So far as the police service is concerned, we should never underestimate the importance of mature police officers, walking the streets and acting as community leaders, organisers and activists, taking a contemporary approach to policing our changing society. They must lead by the power of example not by the example of power and impose minimum standards of behaviour on our streets and must be the friend of the law-abiding, silent majority, and the adversary of the persistent criminal minority.

The transition from traditional to contemporary community policing must be addressed when recruiting and training officers for a more proactive approach to the prevention of antisocial and criminal behaviour and the diversion of young people, from such behaviour, rather than a reactive service of limited police resources chasing unlimited public demand.

When considering the community leadership responsibilities of street police officers towards social improvement, community renewal and social justice, we should consider the more contemporary approach of the Chief of Police, Houston, Texas (USA) in the following extract from the book *Reinventing Government* by David Osbourne and Ted Gaebler, published by the Penguin Group (USA)(1993) entitled *Neighbourhood Oriented Policing* which said:

"In 1982 Lee Brown became Chief of Police in Houston, Texas, a police force beset by charges of racism and brutality. Brown, who was black, set out to transform the force and chose 'Neighbourhood Oriented Policing' the notion that police should help neighbourhoods solve the problems that underlie crime. He assigned most officers to neighbourhood beats and told them to build strong relationships. What they were doing was redefining the role of the patrol officer, to be a community organiser, a community activist, a problem solver. The idea was to make public safety a community responsibility rather than the sole responsibility of the professionals."

However, the British police are no stranger to the concept of community policing and many police forces have introduced many schemes over the years. However, democratic community policing must be an integral part of the British police culture, policing with the consent of the public, and not introduced and withdrawn at the discretion of senior officers.

The British concept of 'policing with the consent of the public' is a good foundation for any contemporary approach to community policing which involves community organising, community activism or problem solving.

If police officers are to lead from the streets and encourage improved standards of behaviour, on behalf of the law-abiding majority, they must be allowed to use personal initiative and discretion and be released from some of the suffocating bureaucracy of the criminal justice system. They must be given the freedom to demonstrate inspirational, motivational and transformational community leadership and working with other agencies divert wayward young people from the precarious path to criminal and antisocial behaviour to an alternative path to responsible citizenship.

However, as usual, a period of prudent conservative austerity measures always follows a period of profligate socialism and the coalition partners had no option but to reduce the cost of community policing in the short term. This means that the investment for increased community policing will not be available until we reduce our annual budget deficits and our national debt and we are well down the road to economic recovery.

We have no option but to suffer austerity cuts to our public services and the police service cannot be exempt from such reductions. However, these austerity measures could be used as an opportunity to rebuild the service from the bottom up. We should have a programme of amalgamations with fewer police forces and fewer police headquarters and fewer desk-bound senior officers and concentrate scarce resources on more street patrols.

It perhaps needs to be emphasised to the public that the amalgamation of police forces is mainly concerned with the headquarters functions and not community policing. Police Forces are divided into divisions, normally under the command of chief superintendents, and subdivisions, normally under the command of superintendents, which would not be affected. The amalgamation of police forces would not affect the divisional structure but would reduce the number of headquarters and senior officers. The most important aspect of the police structure is the relationship between the local community leaders and the divisional commanders, who make the important decisions about local policing challenges and initiatives.

We must, therefore, cover the ground with experienced and mature police officers with the discretion to work with troubled communities to reduce the incidence of criminal and antisocial behaviour at source. They should be free to use their powers of inspirational leadership to increase public safety, rather than a reactive 'hit and run' service where police officers in cars arrive at the scene of an incident after the 'horse has bolted'.

However, there is only so much that the police service can do to change the personal behaviour of those who indulge in criminal and antisocial behaviour and we know from experience that 'evil happens when good men and women do nothing'. We should, therefore, heed the words of Martin Luther King Jr. when he said, "We will have to repent in this generation, not just for the words and deeds of bad people but for the appalling silence of the good people." That means we must encourage natural community leaders to work with local authorities to change the behaviour of those who indulge in criminal and antisocial behaviour.

There is clearly a need for more contemporary community policing and that means that dedicated community constables must be released from the bureaucracy of the criminal justice system and given the freedom to work as community leaders and community organisers and community activists in the interests of crime prevention and reduction. Those who indulge in antisocial and criminal behaviour, to the detriment of their law-abiding neighbours, the silent majority, must be identified and apprehended by their community constables and made the subject of a social contract with the community to change their negative behaviour.

However, those who indulge in house burglary and violent behaviour must be incarcerated and then rehabilitated. They must not be provided with social security benefits without signing a contract of good behaviour as they are 'biting the hand that feeds them'. It may need to be explained to the perpetrators that on the one hand the hard working, tax-paying, majority are providing them with social security benefits and on the other hand they attack their homes, their cars, their property and their families.

This cannot be allowed to continue. It needs to be made clear to them that they have a duty to their community to change their bad behaviour and that should they do so they will continue to get support from the welfare system. However, local government should provide them with work in the community in return for welfare benefits. No persistent criminals should be allowed to damage their local community and expect to continue to receive welfare benefits. There must be consequences for their behaviour.

The protagonist in this process of contemporary community policing must be inspirational community constables, with obvious leadership qualities and relevant experience, who must work with natural community leaders to achieve social improvement, community renewal and social justice.

However, it needs to be emphasised that the police service alone cannot achieve these social objectives, they must gain the support of natural community leaders, who have the respect of their neighbours, and the significant support of a wide range of local government social services.

The police service must search for those with the potential for community leadership and the capacity to achieve social improvement, community renewal and social justice, whilst accepting that they still must recruit those who can investigate and apprehend and prosecute those serious and violent criminals who have no motivation to change their behaviour.

Nothing that has been said about the need for contemporary community policing arrangements, affects the need for international, national and regional policing arrangements, to deal with the most serious criminals and criminal gangs, who have no regard for police force boundaries.

It is, however, expected that a protracted process of more contemporary community policing throughout the country, will eventually reduce the incidence of antisocial and criminal behaviour and those who indulge in such behaviour and free up scarce police resources to deal with more serious criminals and cross-border serious criminal behaviour. This has become even more important with the 'free movement of people' principle of the European Union (EU), where serious criminals are 'free to roam' across uncontrolled borders of the very many European member states.

Whether we provide traditional or contemporary community policing we must remember that our police officers are the 'good guys' who are our last line of defence against the 'bad guys' and they must have our respect.

However, so far as inspirational community leadership is concerned, whether it is for contemporary community policing or local community leadership, the defining characteristic of a great man or woman is their power to leave a lasting impression and they are far and few between.

CHAPTER 5:

We Need Inspirational Community Leadership

The defining characteristic of a great man is his power to leave a lasting impression

A true leader has the personal confidence to stand alone, the courage to make tough decisions and the patience to listen to the needs of others. He probably does not set out to be a leader but becomes one by the integrity of his intention and the quality of his actions. In the end leaders are much like eagles, they don't flock, you usually find them one at a time. The true greatness of human actions is often measured by the extent to which they inspire others to greater things. Influence is spread by the lengthened shadow of one great person but true leadership must be for the benefit of followers not the enrichment of leaders. The defining characteristic of a great man or woman is their power to leave a lasting impression but we need the power of example, not the example of power, and we should always remember that real greatness, however brief, will last forever!

Thomas Raleigh, Fellow of All Souls College, Oxford, in *Elementary Politics* published by Oxford University Press, 1886, said:

"If we wish to see political power more generally diffused, we must increase the number of public spirited individuals. The ordinary citizen often knows very little of the mechanism of government and is too much at the mercy of officials and professional politicians. The mere possession of a vote does not imply the possession of political power. Party managers must be made to feel that they cannot count on our votes unless their acts are in accordance with the principles to which we adhere."

The following extract from *The Rights of Man* by Jacques Maritan, which was published by Centenary Press in 1913, explains the authority behind enduring political leadership, as follows:

"The aim of society is its own common good, the good of the social body. The common good is the foundation of authority. For leading a community of human persons towards their common good, requires that certain individuals be charged with this guidance and the directions which they determine (should) be followed by other members of the community."

The COPEC Commission Report on Politics and Citizenship, published by Longmans Green and Co in 1924 said:

"In the modern state it is the community that governs. Its officers ought indeed, not merely to follow but to lead, yet the ultimate control rests with the community. The function of the state is the establishment of some moral order, a moral order for which justice is

a convenient name and its authority rests upon this and nothing else...
Democracy only attains its great goals, when its citizens think more
of their duties than their rights." This should be a cardinal message
to our more liberal minded politicians and citizens who are more
concerned with citizen's human rights than their civic duties.

However, political leadership and community
leadership are not mutually exclusive. We have waited too
long for our career politicians to provide inspirational
community leadership and have probably not paid
sufficient attention to the leadership qualities of teachers,
police officers, business people and those who lead
community service clubs, sports and social clubs, youth
clubs, the Scouts, the Cubs, the Beavers, the Girl Guides
and the Brownies and many other sporting, voluntary and
charitable groups.

Whilst we should expect inspirational and motivational
community leadership from our elected representatives, we
can always rely on transformational community leadership
from teachers, police officers, business people, religious
leaders, social entrepreneurs, community organisers,
community activists and volunteer youth workers and
charity workers and the many other 'unsung heroes'
working for the common good in many of our deprived
and dysfunctional communities. The astute political
leaders, who can harness the energy of these selfless
community leaders and organisers and activists, will have
found the key, to open the door, to social improvement,
community renewal and social justice.

We must not diminish the enormous contribution of
our teachers towards the common good. Political demands
to raise educational standards are understandable but too
much criticism of the minority of 'poor teachers' merely

serves to erode the confidence of the teaching profession, making their job more difficult. One thing is certain, educational standards will not be raised by centrally imposed targets, performance measurements and league tables or the dead hand of bureaucracy. We must always give our head teachers and teachers our support, to raise their spirits and give them the confidence to accept their classroom leadership responsibilities. Government ministers, of whatever political persuasion, must understand that they just can't raise educational standards by 'caning the teachers'. However, whilst we must keep politicians out of the classrooms, we must persuade teachers and their unions against partisan political disruption and strike action, where the casualties are the children and their parents.

As a society we must never minimise the community leadership potential of brave police officer, working within the community, in the interests of crime prevention and crime reduction and social harmony. In recent years the public demands on the police service, caused by increased criminal and antisocial behaviour, have created an impersonal mobile emergency response, which has done nothing for the relationship between the police service and the community. It is imperative that we return to democratic community policing, that's policing with the consent of the public, with an emphasis on a more contemporary approach to crime prevention and reduction. Society must support those law-abiding men and women, who have the courage to wear a uniform and walk the streets and confront those who indulge in criminal and antisocial behaviour. In fact we should salute them (and their families) for their public service, which they undertake regardless of the considerable personal dangers.

It serves no useful purpose to provide a professional

law enforcement service, with carefully selected and highly trained officers, capable of reducing debilitating criminal and antisocial behaviour, if we reduce their effectiveness by too much legislation, too much paperwork and too many arbitrary targets, removing their initiative and discretion and restricting them to the station and making them 'strangers to the streets'.

So far as enterprising businessmen and women are concerned, they have an important part to play in community leadership. Sadly, they are often characterised as self-serving individuals, particularly when they are successful, when reality suggests that their personal enterprise results in job creation and wealth creation, producing taxation revenues to finance government institutions, essential public services and welfare provision, to the benefit of their local communities and disadvantaged people.

We must encourage our impressive business entrepreneurs to use their leadership skills to inspire our young people to achieve greater goals and objectives in the complex world of work and in their communities. They must adopt the vision of Headmaster Philip Lawrence, killed at the gates of his school in North London, who believed that it was in raising the aspirations of young people that a redemptive process might begin. He wanted to work with disadvantaged young people of low expectations. He valued them all equally as individuals with enormous potential for good.

Whilst the leadership role of politicians, teachers, police officers and business people is crucial in our eternal search for social improvement, community renewal and social justice, the achievement of such ambitions must grow from the 'fertile soil' of local communities, inspired by natural community leaders, not by the dead hand of bureaucracy. Consequently, socialist governments must get out of the habit of ruling by directives and targets as they preside over a discredited political process, made worse by the parliamentary expenses fiasco. When the socialists get back into power, as they always will, they must reduce their natural instinct to control every aspect of our lives. They must change into facilitators and support natural community leaders to lead from the streets and create a climate conducive with the words of President Abraham Lincoln (USA) who said: *"Government of the People for the People by the People."*

To confirm the importance of natural community leaders, rather than talk-shop politicians and desk-bound bureaucrats, in our search for social justice, we should consider the words of Colonel John Blashford-Snell, a former charismatic military commander, emotionally committed to the leadership of inner-city children, when he said:

"We need young leaders who will be able to communicate and inspire young people in inner-cities. You've got to have leaders with whom they can identify, they've got to look like them, dress like them and even smell like them. They will not be world leaders but they will do a good job."

It is, therefore, imperative that local councillors should identify natural community leaders, such as community organisers, community activists, youth workers, voluntary workers and charity workers, those tireless individuals who have gained the respect and trust of their peer groups. They should then create an environment in which their leadership talents are recognised, respected and utilised for the common good. If elected representatives were able to harness the enthusiasm and enterprise of these impressive natural community leaders and provide them with the tools to do the job, they could have the capacity to transform many of our troubled neighbourhoods into more sustainable communities.

Inspirational community leadership is about encouraging ordinary citizens to achieve extraordinary goals towards social improvement, community renewal and social justice. Just one impressive citizen can make the difference between success and failure in any local community initiative and you don't need to be a councillor to be a community leader.

Whilst councillors have important public duties, community leadership and party politics are not mutually exclusive. Furthermore, you don't need to have been a manager to be a community leader. These impressive individuals may have no management experience whatsoever but may have earned the trust of the local people. The art of effective community leadership includes the ability to win the hearts and minds of their fellow citizens. They need the personal confidence to promote their social vision. They must have the personality to make those around them feel important. They must treat others as they would wish to be treated themselves. They must have the courage to take responsibility for their personal actions and those of their peers. They must have the desire to be inspirational teachers, coaches, mentors and role models and be able to 'open the doors' and 'sow the seeds' for our impressionable young people, who are often searching for inspirational direction in a world of mixed messages.

The following extract from an article in *Management Today*, November 2000, entitled 'Dynamic Leaders with a Social Conscience' by Alexander Garrett, set the scene for social entrepreneurs in our local communities:

"Social entrepreneurs succeed where governments fail. Governments have been unsuccessful dealing with problems in certain communities because they just don't know how to approach them but many social entrepreneurs, who come from these communities, have a vision of what needs to be achieved. There are many individuals who want to change society for the better but they need a little support and encouragement. It is individuals who make things happen, not committees. If you look at the most successful community projects they are run by people with leadership qualities not by committees. Good leadership, in the public sector involves handing power to the people."

Social entrepreneurs often receive no encouragement whatsoever from socialist-minded politicians who concentrate too much political and economic power in Westminster and employ civil servants to tempt near impotent local authorities to bid for government hand-outs, with strings attached, which destroys any hope of creating community spirit and civic pride, based on self-funding and self-determination. We need a massive decentralisation of political and economic power to local government and local councillors, to give them the confidence and the financial clout to locate and harness the energy and enthusiasm of inspirational natural community leaders and enterprising social entrepreneurs and provide them with constructive support. We must provide them with the tools to do the job and they will reward us with social improvement, community renewal and social justice, which is not possible in any other way.

Natural community leaders, community organisers, community activists, youth leaders, voluntary workers and charity workers are the foundation of social improvement, community renewal and social justice. There are also thousands of impressive business and professional people, with a social conscience, who are leaders of existing community service clubs, throughout the country, who could make a bigger contribution to the wellbeing of their local communities, if they were involved in the local government decision making process. However, their involvement in the local political process must be underpinned by legislation or regulation.

When we consider the original purpose of community service clubs, such as Rotary, the Lions and the Round Table, whose members are business and professional people, with a social conscience, it was always intended that they should ascertain the needs of their local communities and take positive action. They were encouraged to take an active interest in the civic, cultural, social and moral welfare of their communities and inspire constructive action to achieve social improvement towards the common good. Whilst it is normally a principle of community service clubs to avoid involvement in partisan politics, it would be against their primary objectives to avoid active involvement in local politics, which is about the process of civil government, civil order and an organised society.

Indeed the objectives of Rotary International include the development of opportunities for service to society in general and local communities in particular. Rotary operates on the principle that 'he who serves must act'. Rotary is not merely a state of mind. The individual Rotarian and the Rotary club must put the theory of community service into practice. It is expected that Rotarians will translate the principles of Rotary into social activity by making themselves an active force in community affairs. In most of the worthwhile civic activities, Rotarians should be found as community leaders. Rotary clubs are urged to assume the responsibility to ascertain the moral and social needs of their local community and to actively and confidently inspire and encourage constructive action through the appropriate (government or non-government) agencies.

The book *Adventure in Service* published by Rotary

International in 1949 said:

> *"Rotarians must be an active force in community affairs. In most worthwhile civic activities members will be found as leaders. Rotary clubs are therefore urged to assume the responsibility of ascertaining the social needs of their local communities and inspire constructive action, the advancement of the best interests of their town or city and the spreading of the spirit of civic pride and loyalty among its citizens."*

So far as the Round Table community service movement is concerned, another international organisation, inspired by the Rotary movement, their original objectives included the need to emphasise that *'one's occupation or vocation offers an excellent medium of service to the community, the need to cultivate the highest ideals in civic traditions, the need to encourage personal integrity in public and private life and the need to stimulate interest in all matters of public concern.'*

The objectives of the International Association of Lions Clubs include the 'need to promote the principles of good government and citizenship, to take an active interest in the civic, cultural, social and moral welfare of the community and to provide a forum for the open discussion of matters of public interest' but any active interest in civic, cultural, social and moral welfare should be done with the support of local government.

The original objectives of the 'Women's Institute' movement included the creation of a powerful national organisation, able to bring some pressure to bear on governments, which would not be disregarded, and to develop a campaign of social, civic and political education. The Townswomen's Guilds, which were founded in 1929 to educate women in the principles of good citizenship, actively campaigns on social issues and is a force for social improvement and community renewal. The Mothers Union is an organisation of over 3.6 million people, operating in 77 countries, which believes in the importance of families. The Women's Royal Voluntary Service (WRVS) which helps thousands of older people get more out of their lives by providing services in their homes in hospitals and in the community, such as the 'meals on wheels' service. There is no doubt that the leaders of these impressive women's voluntary groups could have a massive influence within local government, towards the achievement of enduring social improvement, community renewal and social justice.

However, the greatest influence on social improvement, community renewal and social justice must be educational leadership. We must expand the development of transformational community schools and inspirational head teachers and teachers. We must also emphasise the importance of moral education, character training, socialisation training, vocational training, sporting excellence and education for citizenship in school programmes. These subjects must be given equal status with more academic subjects in the school curriculum, as nothing is more important than education of our young people for employment and citizenship.

The road to citizenship passes by the schoolhouse and onto the streets but before our teachers can teach our children the values on which our civilisation depends, we must remove undisciplined classroom behaviour, which is described in an article entitled 'The Blackboard Jungle' which was published in the *Options Magazine*, 7 February 1997 as follows:

"The Nation's schools are in crisis and our children in a state of terminal moral decline and, especially if you are a parent, it's all the

fault of the teachers. The truth is that few of us know what it's really like being a teacher, to stand up in front of a class of fifteen-year-olds, to be spat at, sworn at, even physically abused, before you can begin doing the job you're paid to do. So far this term I've been assaulted three times. My name is Joanna Oldham. I was an English teacher. My birth certificate says I'm twenty-eight, yet I feel about ninety. I'm simply done in. After four years in two state-run secondary schools, I've had enough. There's so much general chaos in every class that most of it goes unreported. It's more like crowd control than teaching."

More than a decade after the New Labour mantra 'Education, Education, Education', did we get calm and disciplined classrooms, conducive with teaching and learning? Well not if the following extract from an article in the *Daily Mail*, 15 April 2007, entitled 'Anarchy in Class' by Carl Storm, a former operational soldier, is anything to go by:

"Teaching is not meant to be a physically dangerous profession, coping with threats of violence and risks of hospitalisation. Well in some of our inner cities those are the problems teachers face on a daily basis. Thanks to the complete breakdown in authority and discipline, too many schools are now places of naked fear, with staff left at the mercy of thugs, who have neither manners nor morals. Handling aggression, foul-mouthed abuse and raw belligerence have become an integral part of the classroom routine. While inner city schools are gripped by chaos, the authorities pretend that they have never been doing better… But those of us who have worked in the system know better. No one could come from a tougher background than me, yet I have to say that I would not dream of sending children of mine to an English state school. I would rather crawl through broken glass, than inflict such a punishment on them."

When some of our community schools are out of

control, often caused by a few disruptive pupils, and the teachers cannot maintain an environment conducive with teaching and learning, then the authorities must enforce school discipline. Teachers will have many qualities, mainly concerned with the delivery of lessons, rather than the maintenance of discipline. Consequently, the authorities should employ former police officers, with the strength of character to create an environment of discipline, which would benefit the teaching and learning experience. Former streetwise police officers would have the maturity and courage and experience to deal with awkward, aggressive and violent young people. Their presence at the back of the classrooms, in the corridors and on the playgrounds, would encourage a calming influence on the children and young people.

Furthermore, some of our children and young people have some difficulty understanding some academic subjects and are made to feel a failure and it is understandable that they may play truant or may behave badly in the classroom. Some of them are just not academically inclined but they may have a vocational or sporting bent. Wouldn't it then be sensible to let them major on a sport such as football, cricket or athletics or major on a vocational subject such as plumbing, joinery or car maintenance? If they were able to major on a sporting or vocational subject, something that interested them, the deal would be that they would also take an interest in certain academic subjects such as English or maths or history. In other words, teachers would concentrate on what they were good at and what interested them and not pursue what they are bad at and worried about.

Whilst inspirational educational leadership has the greatest influence on the wellbeing of our children and young people, enterprising business leadership is crucial to complete the journey from the home, through the school and to the workplace. There is no point in the educational process, if it does not prepare our young people for the world of work, and there is no point in preparing them for the world of work if there are no jobs and there will only ever be enough jobs if enterprising and entrepreneurial business people create those jobs. Local business leadership is crucial to the success of our communities and the wellbeing of our young people.

We must never underestimate the impact that impressive businessmen and women can have upon our impressionable young people, particularly when they venture into the world of work. Furthermore, make no mistake, regardless of their loose rhetoric, politicians do not create jobs in private business, business people do. In fact, socialist Labour politicians often make it difficult for business people to create jobs due to their obsession with over-regulation and excessive taxation. However, nothing will stop entrepreneurs from creating businesses and new employment and paying taxation to finance the government machine, essential public services and welfare benefits, which are a bottomless pit. Labour governments always create unaffordable government institutions and essential public services and welfare distribution, financed through punitive taxation on private enterprise, which reduces investment and growth and new employment.

The contribution to society of small businessmen (and women) was recognised in a government publication entitled *Report of the Committee of Inquiry on Small Firms*, published by HMSO in 1971, which said:

"The contribution of small businessmen (and women) to the vitality of society is inestimable. The qualities of vigour, enterprise and ambition, which characterise so many of them, have made them natural community leaders and they have been benefactors to their localities which makes life more meaningful and pleasant."

Furthermore, remember the words of John Mackay, the CEO of the Whole Foods Supermarkets (USA) when he said: *"Business people are truly the heroes, they are the value creators in the world and they lift humanity out of poverty and create prosperity."*

The book *World Class* by Rosabeth Moss Kanter, published by Simon and Schuster, New York, 1995, had this to say under the title 'Business Leadership in the Community':

"Around the world movements are emerging to get businesses to take more responsibility for solving (community) problems. If government is unable to solve social problems, many say business should accept the challenge. One of the issues is a crisis in leadership. I still think that governments need to be guardians of the infrastructure but those best suited to do that are smart enough to stay away from politics. Many people with a desire to serve their communities think they will do it through their companies."

If the authorities want enterprising business people and professional people to get involved in politics, they must change their preference for professional politicians. Professional politicians with no professional or business experience often become out of touch with the real world outside of the Westminster village. Parliamentary democracy cannot thrive with insular politicians, with no business or professional experience, working with desk-bound civil servants, who often have meetings about meetings.

If the authorities want to encourage business people to demonstrate their community leadership, then encourage them to employ able-bodied young people who are currently paid social security benefits to stay in bed and do nothing. Supporting idleness and creating a dependency culture is bad for the individuals concerned and bad for the community. The authorities should give incentives to enterprising business people to create new jobs and provide employment security, not social welfare security, for those who exist on benefits. We must get indolent young people back to work and off the streets, if we are to dismantle the street gang culture, the drugs culture, the gun and knife culture and the binge drinking culture. Welfare benefits must not be a lifestyle choice for idle young people who are paid to do nothing and free to work on the black market or lead a life of crime, which is effectively biting the benevolent hand that feeds them.

Sadly, socialist Labour governments are in the habit of imposing punitive taxation on industrious people and giving it to those who are strangers to work. A more liberal conservative approach would be to reduce punitive National Insurance taxation on manual jobs, so that business people can create manual work for the unqualified work-shy. They would be forced out to work (or lose their benefits) where they would learn the benefits of regular time-keeping, hard manual work, self-respect, self-sufficiency and gain the respect of their extended families and friends and communities.

Whilst political, educational, business and community leadership are important ingredients in the goal for social improvement, community renewal and social justice it will come to nothing, without inspirational community policing leadership. However, there are many new challenges facing the criminal justice system and the police service, which perhaps need a more contemporary approach to traditional community policing.

We must do whatever is necessary to encourage those responsible for the provision of police services, to accept the need for more contemporary community policing and the community leadership potential of dedicated community constables, well beyond the limitations of a law enforcement agency. The government must get off the backs of street police officers and trust them to use their strength of character and their powers of persuasion and their personal discretion and initiative to change adverse behaviour on our streets and neighbourhoods. They must be trained to act as role models, mentors, community organisers, community activists, and lead our more awkward young people from the path to criminality.

However, street police officers must be actively supported by their local authorities and they must not be left to walk alone. The authorities must provide a range of youth support services and attractive facilities to get our more difficult young people off the streets. They must also invest in inspirational community constables to change the adverse behaviour of some of our more difficult young people in our eternal search for social improvement, community renewal and enduring social justice.

Furthermore, if community policing is to be effective, it is imperative that the police service, supported by the criminal justice system, breaks the repetitive cycle of crime, committed by a minority of recidivist criminals, which damages the effectiveness of the police service and swamps the criminal courts, the probation service and the prison service. The long-term incarceration of habitual criminals, with no motivation to reform, is in the interest of public safety and security, pending vocational training and community work on release, as opposed to long-term benefits and state dependency of those persistent criminals who are unemployable.

Whilst political, educational, business, policing and natural community leadership are essential building blocks to achieve a better society, which is often described as a secular society, the whole system should probably be underpinned by religious beliefs. However, our religious leaders must avoid divisive extremism and fundamentalism, which is practiced by a minority of vociferous individuals, particularly in the Muslim religion.

Those who seek moral standards from sources other than religion should consider the following extract from the book entitled *The Secularisation of the European Mind in the Nineteenth Century*, which was written by Owen Chadwick and published in 1975:

"Morality never has been separated from religion and those who undertook to provide a system of morality which would have no links with religion had a task of exceptional difficulty if they were to make a system of morality which would touch the conscience of a large number of ordinary people."

When one considers the religious conflict which exists in the world today, caused mainly by religious fundamentalism, the time has come to unite around a liberal approach to religion, which believes that people should enjoy individual freedom, liberty and conscience in spiritual matters and that there should be no pressure to conform to a particular religion and that we should be tolerant of those who follow a different path to faith.

The Unitarian Church, which was founded by a group of non-conformist English Presbyterians in 1662, is a 'spiritual community who encourage you to think for yourself and is not bound by religious fundamentalism and dogma. They are religious liberals who affirm that people should enjoy individual liberty and private judgement in spiritual matters. They believe that the authority for your faith lies within your own conscience and they impose no pressure to conform and they respect and tolerate those who follow a different path to religious faith.'

The purpose of the Unitarian congregation is to 'meet

the spiritual needs of individuals in a loving community; to share joy and offer comfort in times of trial; to enjoy the warmth of fellowship and to make itself welcoming, inclusive and a blessing to the wider world. They find their bond of unity in shared values such as the nurture of the spiritual dimension; the use of reason and honest doubt in the search for truth; mutual respect and goodwill in personal relationships; constructive tolerance and openness towards sincerely held beliefs of others; peace, compassion, justice and democracy in human affairs; and reverence for the earth and the natural system of which we are part.'

The world would be a better place, if our religious leaders could reject religious intolerance and embrace religious liberalism, practiced by the Unitarian Church, and were tolerant of the sincerely held beliefs of others, which doesn't appear to be the case in the Islamic tradition.

Furthermore, the government could pay thousands of farmers, through the welfare budget, to take on one or more young unemployed people and teach them the value of hard work. Farmers are normally independent minded people, wedded to the world of hard work. They are definitely not nine-to-five, desk-bound bureaucrats. Recent years have seen a decline in agricultural production and many farmers have diversified to survive. Farmers are respected members of their communities and they never suffer fools gladly. They could be ideal mentors to our young people, if they accepted the challenge to teach them the importance of agricultural production, respect for animal welfare and concern for the environment. Working in the fields, exposed to the elements, feeding the farm animals, milking the cows, grooming and exercising the horses and operating farm machinery under the supervision of pragmatic and industrious farmers, could be a life changing experience for our young people and an essential alternative source of income for many hard-pressed farmers.

The main provider of 'citizenship services' could be the military, which would be much more beneficial to the wellbeing of our country than fighting wars, which have nothing to do with our national security. We are proud of our armed forces and brave soldiers and the world would be a much better place if they were committed to defending our national interests and security, not fighting questionable wars. If we involved our brave soldiers in youth projects, they could demonstrate the benefits of discipline, leadership, teamwork, hard work, long hours, duties and responsibilities and inspirational leadership in this complex world of confused messages. This is similar to the 'National Citizen Service' initiative which was announced at the Conservative Party Annual Conference in 2007 and hopefully has been actively pursued.

Furthermore, the British Police Service, which was founded on military discipline and leadership, could play an important role in the supervision of community support work in deprived or troubled communities. This community support work could be undertaken by retired police officers, employed on short-term contracts, working with social entrepreneurs, community organisers and community activists, involved in the rewarding vocation of helping those citizens who are less fortunate than themselves.

No young person should leave school or further education destined for a life on benefits, with no job, no money and no hope. No young person should leave any form of incarceration, destined for a life on the streets, with no alternative to criminal and antisocial behaviour and working on the black market. Every unemployed or unemployable young person, regardless of their social background, should be given some form of community work, when they leave education, in return for benefits.

We must get out of the socialist habit of supporting disadvantaged citizens with a 'cheque in the post' and 'free to roam' and 'no strings attached'. We do disadvantaged citizens no favours by giving them something for nothing. This is particularly the case with those criminals who receive their benefits from the taxpayers and then break into their houses or steal their cars. The receipt of social benefits should create an obligation to the beneficiaries to give something back to the community.

The unemployed and even the unemployable should be given the opportunity to live and work on thousands of farms, supervised and mentored by farmers and farm managers. They could also undertake disciplined outdoor physical activities, such as mountaineering and sailing and outward-bound, under the direction of charismatic military or ex-military leaders. They could also undertake community support work, in our deprived and troubled communities, supporting the elderly and the disabled and the disadvantaged under the supervision of mature community constables and former police officers and supported by inspirational community organisers and activists and volunteers.

Furthermore, the leasing of county council farms for those who cannot afford to purchase agricultural land should be given greater importance by central and regional and local government. For more than 100 years county council farms, which were established in the 1890s, have been providing exciting opportunities for young people to enter agriculture. The initiative took off after the First World War because of concern for food security and a desire to provide a livelihood for returning soldiers. Since then, new entrants have started out on a council smallholding and gradually built their business and experience. Because of the significant capital requirements of agriculture it is a very difficult industry to enter without significant support. By 1926 the county farms estate had reached 29,532 holdings. The Agriculture Act 1970 demanded a reorganisation of the council farm estate, leading to the consolidation and enlarging of existing holdings, a process which has continued ever since, ensuring that the farms are of a viable size in modern day agriculture.

Sadly the recent economic recession meant that some council's started to sell off of their county farms to fill the deep holes in their budgets and this process needs to be reversed when the economy recovers. In 2010 Somerset County Council decided to sell off two thirds of its 60 tenanted farms, despite strong opposition from stakeholders. A year later (2011), Gloucestershire County Council followed suit, approving the sale of 43% of its tenanted farms in a bid to raise £125 million in capital receipts. North Yorkshire pursued a similar policy as each of its 48 farms become vacant. Apparently, since 1964, the council farms estate across England and Wales has shrunk by 79% to just 3,442 holdings and this effectively means fewer opportunities for new entrants to get that important first foothold on the farming ladder. However, it's not all bad news as some county councils are now actively investing in their council farm estates.

Whilst this is an egalitarian approach to agricultural land redistribution, it would not be unreasonable for local government to requisition land from substantial landowners to extend their county council farm estates. This would mean that thousands of young people would get to operate county council tenanted farms or small-holdings and they could be mentored by the management of the landowners providing the land.

No one should doubt the ability of an army of soldiers and former soldiers, police officers and retired officers and independent minded farmers, to move young people from unemployment and antisocial and criminal behaviour, towards a more positive and productive lifestyle.

Finally, our country needs the devolution of economic power to the lowest practical level on the premise that *'democracy grows from the bottom up and dies from the top-down'* and that *'government's should only do for the people, what they can't do for themselves'* and that *'we can't wait for great visions from great people because they are in short supply'* and that *'we must light our own small fires in the darkness'*.

Conclusion

Having suffered thirteen years of big-spending socialism under the guise of New Labour, we again found ourselves in an economic mess, with the biggest national debt crisis in peacetime history. The electorate were deceived by the warm words of Anthony Charles Lynton Blair, leader of the New Labour project, which was never more than a political pretence, influenced by President Clinton's 'triangulation' idea, to achieve and retain power. Whilst the' triangulation' idea promoted policies which were unfamiliar to socialism, such as smaller government, deregulation and balanced budgets, it was sufficient to get them back into power. Not surprisingly, they later took the opposite approach of 'top-down' control, over-regulation, excessive borrowing and reckless spending, under the influence of a self-proclaimed 'prudent' Chancellor, Gordon Brown.

Whilst Prime Minister Blair was a political enigma, and many thought he was more conservative than socialist, he was a cover for many ministers, who supported communism when younger, and for their socialist militant trade union leader comrades who needed to '*keep the red flag flying*'.

The reality was, however, that most of these socialist dreamers, who were born out of trade unionism and communism, had never run anything in their lives, let alone large government departments, which they were not qualified to lead. What they did, however, was impose their militant and divisive socialist agenda onto our liberal western democracy and drag our country into the economic gutter, as they did in the dreaded 'Winter of Discontent', when we were described as the 'Poor Man of Europe'.

However, the biggest culprit for the damage to our economy was the former Chancellor and unelected Prime Minister, Gordon Brown, who initially stuck with the Conservative spending plans but then went on a tax, borrow and spend binge. He created unaffordable public services and welfare entitlements and public sector pensions and a national debt legacy. He also sold off our gold reserves at the bottom of the market and raided private pension schemes and damaged the pension expectations of those who were saving for their retirement, whilst protecting the gold-plated, index-linked, pensions of public sector workers and politicians.

Incidentally, talking about damaged private pension schemes, this is what Ros Altman had to say about the terminal damage done to our private pension schemes by New Labour, reported by Alex Brummer, in his book entitled *The Great Pensions Robbery: How New Labour betrayed retirement* published by Random House Business Books in 2010:

"This Chancellor (Gordon Brown) will go down in history as the one who destroyed our (private) pension system... He clearly decided pension funds were a ripe target but this was irresponsible government. It put final salary schemes at risk. They warned this would happen and the predictions have come true. Brown knowingly destroyed what was once one of the great pension systems in the world and he did it deliberately."

It also said: *"One of the architects of the tax change (was) Ed Balls."*

Furthermore, as Chancellor, he supported Prime Minister Blair's five foreign wars, particularly the controversial Iraq War, which he could have opposed, and spent billions of pounds on military campaigns which appeared to have little to do with our national security or national interests. In fact, Iraq is now in such turmoil, with the emergence of the barbaric Islamic State (IS) jihadist terrorists, that we should consider whether our military campaign was responsible for an explosion of Islamic fundamentalist jihadist terrorism throughout the region.

Whilst our country already had a national debt burden, our unelected Prime Minister, Gordon Brown, approached the 2010 General Election with the proposal that we should spend our way out of recession, through public sector investment, presumably with more borrowed money, rather than public sector austerity measures, designed to bring down recurring annual budget deficits, which he alleged would hit the poorest hardest. He also said that the stark choice facing the electorate was between New Labour investment and Conservative imposed austerity measures.

His second line of attack was to indulge in the 'politics of envy' and he emerged as an old socialist 'class warrior' attacking the 'privileged' backgrounds of the opposition leaders and their attendance at public schools, when many of his own cabinet ministers had experienced similar privileged backgrounds and attended similar public schools. He cynically said at the despatch box, that the Conservative opposition had dreamed up their policies on the playing fields of Eton. This childish and negative 'class warfare' rhetoric confirmed his former neo-Marxist credentials.

We were again consumed with the 'politics of envy' from old Labour 'class warriors', many of whom supported communism when younger. They were supported by their militant trade union leader comrades who habitually criticise 'privileged' Conservatives for attending top public schools, rather than what are known as 'bog-standard' comprehensives.

Furthermore, whilst New Labour and their trade union leader comrades were always consumed with the 'politics of envy' and 'class warfare' and schemed to get rid of the House of Lords and the Hereditary Peers, when their chance came, their hypocrisy knew no bounds. They simply got rid of many 'privileged' and 'upper-class' Hereditary Peers to make way for old and New Labour politicians, their political advisors, party activists, trade union leaders and wealthy financial donors in the upper chamber.

So far as the British economy is concerned, those old enough to have suffered the militant trade union strikes of the 1970s, which culminated in the 'Winter of Discontent', when refuse bins were not being emptied and dead bodies were not being buried and the lights went out, will know that the socialist trade unions brought down a Conservative Government.

We later suffered the miners' strike of 1984/85, when the socialist miner's union leadership tried to bring down another Conservative Government but they hadn't accounted for Prime Minister, Margaret Thatcher, and the British Police Service, who had prepared for such an eventuality. No government, of whatever colour, can concede to any group of workers who are trying to bring down a democratically elected government?

The main conclusion of the past thirty years is that profligate socialism, financed from the fruits of capitalism, does not work and we must now question, whether our country is governable, with a major political party financed by militant trade union leader barons. In fact, without the money from the trade unions the Labour Party would probably be bankrupt.

Well the electorate expressed their opinion at the 2010 General Election and they rejected big-spending socialism under the guise of New Labour and their militant socialist trade union leader paymasters and voted for liberating liberal conservatism in the form of a coalition government. The coalition partners then buried their differences and worked together in a spirit of compromise in the national interest and for the common good.

Incidentally, the message from the 2014 Liberal Democratic, Party Conference, was a 'Stronger Economy' and a 'Fairer Society' which could have been mistaken for a message from a Conservative Party Conference. However, their leaders, who are ministers in the coalition government, wasted no time to attack their coalition partners. They would have got more electoral credibility had they emphasised their minority contribution to coalition governance, which was based upon compromise, rather than attacking their coalition partners. If they really believed in a 'Stronger Economy' and a 'Fairer Society' they should have supported their coalition partners, who had worked to achieve a stronger economy, which will eventually result in more investment into a fairer society.

Our choice at the 2015 General Election is between Conservatives, who would instinctively maintain fiscal discipline and balanced budgets and reduced immigration, as opposed to Labour which has a track-record of wrecking the economy and is in denial about their contribution to our immigration problems. We also have choices between the Conservatives, who will attempt to reform our relationship with the EU and provide an in-out referendum and the United Kingdom Independence Party

(UKIP), which exists to leave the EU but can't provide a referendum and Labour, which wants to remain in the EU, regardless of our concerns, and won't provide a referendum, unless it becomes politically expedient to do so.